CONTENTS

PROLOGUE

I am standing in front of the Karmic Board in the Bardo State, which is the state of readiness for reincarnation. I am relaxed, but excited because I am ready to learn from my mentors on the board, what I overcame during my previous life and what I need to accomplish in my next lifetime. They will review my past lives with me and show me areas I need to strengthen for my soul's growth. Because I have free will, they ask me if I agree. I do and am very eager to hear what they recommend for me.

First of all, I will be born into a wealthy southern family to challenge their bigoted traditions. It will be difficult because they are wealthy and feel entitled to their powerful position in the stratified southern society transferred from Europe and the British Isles.

I must endure rejection, betrayal, abandonment and the resultant guilt and loneliness because of my plan but will grow spiritually if I rise above those challenges, not blaming, but forgiving all the teachers in my life who are there to show me the way.

I will experience the pain of drug and alcohol addiction in the heart of my family. It will be the catalyst for me to search beyond the obvious causes of dependency and plumb the depths of the emotional and spiritual attitudes of each person, delving into their fears and releasing them.

My mission will be to heal myself and others through the many and varied personal and educational experiences that I will find. I will spend my life studying and learning from many different healers, some gifted spiritually and others merely charlatans. My soul will lead me.

Over time I will become aware of motivational patterns of behavior that all people develop. My assignment will be to show and explain each pattern to each seeker. With their new awareness, unlimited possibilities will become available. Their ultimate gift will be peace and change for their highest and best good.

And finally, my personal overall goal will be to open my heart to the universal truths and make them mine for my soul's development, thus standing strong in the truth forever. I will accept my given name of Jeanne.

A baby is God's opinion that life should go on.
Carl Sandburg

1. A TRAUMATIC BEGINNING

1936

NELL

It was hot, Florida hot that was so humid that Nell's light cotton maternity dress stuck to her body. Every pore in her body was dripping perspiration causing her embarrassment. Southern ladies weren't supposed to show any outward signs of bodily functions like sweat. She dabbed at her face with one hand as she glanced quickly into her rear-view mirror. Gracious, what will my darling doctor think about me looking so damp? Nell asked herself. She opened the little window in the front of her car door to let a little air blow on her. That's better, she thought as the air fluffed her hair. Horrors, I certainly don 't want to look windblown, she thought and closed the tiny window a little, only allowing a small portion of air to enter her car.

The parking spaces in front of Dr. Matthew Symington's office were empty when she arrived. She parked and walked slowly into the doctor's office. Surprised that there were several other women in his waiting room all fanning themselves for comfort. She thought, smugly, They obviously can't afford a car, not too well off. The small black fans, one on the nurse's desk and one by her chair were running, but the difference the tiny blades on the fans made was negligible. Nell hesitated to use her fan, it seemed so common.

"The doctor will see you, now, Mrs. Greenfield," his friendly nurse called.

"Thank you, Ida," Nell said, giving her a superficial nod and smile and swept into the doctor's office.

Matthew stood up, came around his desk and said, "You are looking well, Nell, considering the tragic death of your dear father. I will miss him."

"It's been a blow to me and the whole family. I didn't think he would leave so soon."

"How have you been sleeping?"

"Not well, and of course my condition doesn't make it any easier for me to rest properly," "Let's check you over. I'll call Ida during the examination."

"Well, Matthew, how am I?" Nell inquired after she returned to his office from the exam room.

"Everything looks good. You need to get plenty of rest and watch the sweets. I'll see you next month. Take it easy driving, Nell. You seem a little agitated."

"I have good reason because of my mourning, but I always drive well. You know me." "Yes, I certainly do know you, Nell," Matthew replied.

Imagine him intimating that I won 't drive safely, she thought, as she turned the car and drove out onto the country road to home.

What was she going to do, now that she couldn't see her father anymore? He had loved and trusted her. She was his little Nell who could do nothing wrong. Her sisters sometimes said she was spoiled, but her father didn't think so. He just loved to make her happy and had the money to do it. He had given her a trust fund full of securities that had made her wealthy in her own right. She began to cry thinking about never seeing him again and accelerated as she was sobbing. She was short, she could barely see above the dashboard. Driving a Cadillac, surely everyone will make way.

The country road she was traveling on turned sharply and as she flew around the bend, she felt the car's wheel wrenched out of her hands and her body tumbling, tumbling, tumbling until everything went black.

Leroy Mason came around the corner in his truck and slowed down because of his load of hay he was taking to a customer for his horse. "My gosh," he said, slamming on his squeaky brakes. "Lookie there, Skeeter," he said to his dog riding in back with his load as he jumped out of his truck. "There's someone in that there car." He peered in the window and saw Nell, her body twisted and traumatized, lying in the front seat with one of her feet stuck in the little open window in the driver's door. "She's out cold, I hope she's alive." Leroy carefully extricated her from the car, carried her to his truck, laid her on the front seat and slid in, putting her head in his lap and drove to the hospital as carefully and quickly as he could.

When Neal got the call from the hospital that his wife was there after a car accident, he drove as fast as he dared, rushed to the hospital, and was met by the attending doctor.

"Is my wife, okay? Did she lose the baby? Neal asked demanding an answer.

"It's a miracle that they are both fine. That baby of yours is not coming out until it is good and ready," the doctor said, making a little joke.

"I'm so glad, doctor. My wife and I have just been married for a short while and this baby is my first child."

"We'll keep your wife for a few days to make sure everything is all right. Don't you worry, things look good. Why don't you go see her, now. She's fully awake."

Knocking on the private room with a big bunch of roses

for his Nell, Neal gave them to the private nurse who was attending his wife. "How are you, dear? You had quite a near miss."

"It was, but I don't want anyone to know about it. Just tell our friends that the doctor put me in the hospital to make sure my pregnancy was going well and I'll be home in a few days."

"Have the maid bring me some clean clothes and my make-up. I don't want any visitors and when I leave, I want to look my best in case I run into anyone. I don't want anyone saying they saw me, and I looked terrible."

"Now, go and leave me, dear. I want to rest so I can get back to my lovely self, again," Nell said, holding her arms out for Neal to reach over and give her a kiss and a hug."

After he left, Nell lay in bed, sore and bruised all over, wishing she felt better and wasn't pregnant. Her belly was getting larger all the time. I'll be glad when this baby comes. I know Neal wants a boy as an heir. It was the right thing to do. My mother told me I was duty bound to produce at least one offspring for him. I can't imagine what those two other wives of his were thinking, not giving him one baby. Well, he divorced them and married me. I don 't intend to disappoint him, she thought, turned over on her side and shut her eyes for an afternoon nap.

When Neal came to take her home, the private nurse, Neal had immediately hired had spent a great deal of time, helping Nell get dressed, fixing her hair and eve putting a little blush on her cheeks.

Every day, Nell carefully inspected her legs for any signs of phlebitis. Once was more than enough to let that happen to her, again. Who would have thought having a baby would cause that. She certainly didn't. She thought back eight years ago when she was twenty-one and was crowned Queen of Gasparilla and was so innocent. Nell smiled when she thought about all the proposals she had before she accepted Winton Taylor. How did I not know he was a terrible alcoholic? It was like a nightmare being married to that man. Perhaps, that was why I was bedridden with phlebitis for a year after my little Nell Leigh was born.

Neal got her another car and encouraged her to drive again. At first it was hard to do, she was so nervous, but soon she felt comfortable behind the wheel. Nell didn't reform, she drove like a bat out of hell the rest of her life.

Nell hadn't felt well for a week or so, having little twinges. She decided to go see

Matthew to make sure everything was alright. He said she was just tuning-up to have her baby. A few days later, Nell knew her concerns had been right when her labor pains started a little after midnight. She woke Neal and said it was time to go.

He drove her to the Tampa Bay Hospital where she spent the wee hours in labor. Jeanne arrived at 11:11 AM on September 10th, 1936, a beautiful little baby girl, perfect in every way except one. She had little malformed feet.

Many years later, Jeanne learned from a numerologist that her time of birth added up to 911, the national emergency number that is used for all emergencies. Jeanne was to spend a lot of her adult life taking friends and family to the hospital.

Coming out to the waiting room, Dr. Symmes found Neal and said, "Congratulations, Neal," with a big smile on his face as he shook Neal's hand.

"Have a cigar, doctor and thanks for all you did for Nell and our baby girl. Nell and I decided if we had a girl, we were going to name her Jeanne, using the French spelling. My first name is John or Jean in French. The feminine is Jeanne.',

"That's a beautiful name for a beautiful little girl. There is one thing I want to discuss with you and Nell when Nell has recovered. Jeanne needs her legs and feet braced right away, so they will develop correctly. It will gradually correct the problem with her feet. It's essential we do it. Otherwise, your baby will have years of pain trying to walk on her little feet. You wouldn't want that, would you?"

Neal replied, "No, that would be terrible. I will discuss it with Nell, right away.

"Good, now go see your beautiful baby in the nursery and your lovely wife."

Neal stopped at the flower shop for more roses, Nell's favorite flowers. He found the nursery and asked the nurse to hold the Greenfield baby up for him to see. "She's very pretty," he said, with a big smile.

He found Nell in the white silk bed jacket he had given her when she told him she was pregnant. "Hello, Nell," he said, handing the flowers to the private nurse he had hired and said, "I'd like to be alone with my wife for a moment."

When the nurse had left, Neal said, "You look wonderful considering you just had our baby girl. I saw her. She's beautiful."

"I'm glad you like her, "Nell replied, smiling at her handsome husband.

Neal pulled up a visitor's chair next to Nell's bed and reached for her hand. She smiled at him, pleased that it was all over.

When Neal brought up the subject of their daughter's feet, she wouldn't even discuss it with him. When the doctor tried to talk to her about it, she said she'd give it some thought, but secretly she thought, I don 't have any intention of doing that. It would mean I would be tied down having to spend a lot more time caring for the baby and miss all my social life. Besides, my friends would whisper behind my back that Nell had had a malformed child. I can't have my friends thinking that.

A week later when they left the hospital, the nurse sat in the back seat with the baby. Nell had hired her to take care of Baby Jeanne until she could hire a nanny.

Nell couldn't wait to get back into her clothes again, go to luncheons and dinner parties, play bridge with her friends and resume her social life. She had been dreaming about it for months.

She interviewed and hired a negro nanny, named Aida, to take care of Jeanne. Her friends had recommended Aida by name, touting her praises. Nell took their advice. Her friends could be trusted. Nell didn't intend to tell Aida that she came so highly recommended. Nell didn't want her to get any uppity ideas.

Nell waited until Neal came home from the bank where he was president and said,

"Neal, I've hired a nanny named Aida to look after Jeanne and also cook and clean for us."

"Good, now you can take trips with me and won't be tied down. Is this negro girl, trustworthy with children?"

"She comes recommended by my friends. I'll watch and make sure she does what is expected of her."

Jeanne was to be blessed with a loving nanny whose kindness, and fun-loving ways would influence Jeanne the rest of her life.

Aida was given a small alcove to sleep in near Jeanne's nursery at night on the other side of the house. Nell didn't intend to listen to a crying baby. Before Aida was hired, Nell had outlined her duties that were expected of her. In the morning, Aida was to be up by six o'clock and have breakfast ready for Neal before he left for the bank. She was to perform cleaning the house, cooking the meals and doing the laundry and ironing in around the baby's schedule. Nell told her the outside work would be done by a hired hand.

Each day when Nell arose, sometimes early, sometimes later, depending on her social schedule for the day, she instructed Aida as to what her duties were for the day.

"Are we clear as to your duties?" Nell asked Aida every day.

"Yes, I understand, missus. I take Miss Jeanne out for some air after I get dinner started and clean up the kitchen?" She said, holding Jeanne in her arms.

"Be sure, the kitchen is spotless, and I don't want any of your relatives coming round for a hand-out, understand?"

"Yes, misses," Aida replied. She took Jeanne to give her a bottle and a bath. When she had finished and Baby Jeanne was back in her bed, sound asleep for her morning nap, Aida worked as fast as she could so she could take Jeanne out for a stroll in her beautiful baby carriage.

"Baby, I hear you," Aida said, as she took the stairs to Jeanne's nursery two at a time.

"We're going outside," Aida said, lifting Jeanne out of her little crib and hugging her. "I love you, baby girl. I love you like you were my own," tickling Jeanne's tummy.

When Jeanne started gurgling with glee, Aida said, "Let's go out and see our friends." She changed Jeanne and dressed her up in one of Jeanne's dozens of little outfits, her aunts had given her. "Here we go, sugar," Aida said, holding Jeanne in her arms and hurrying carefully downstairs with her. "Now, don't cry when I put you in your carriage. We're going for a walk."

Aida hurried outside, carefully dropping the carriage down the four white stairs, to walk around the property. As soon as the carriage began moving, Jeanne became quiet. She gurgled and made little noises looking up at Aida.

"Hear them noises, baby? That's the birdies talking to each other, did you know that?"

Every day when the weather was nice, Aida and Jeanne would go out to enjoy the day. When Jeanne outgrew the carriage, Aida would prop her up in a special little wagon, and pull her around the property, to see the flowers and birds. One of their favorite places was the pond where the majestic white swans swam gracefully around in the water. The pond also attracted birds and animals year-round. Jeanne and Aida would sit and watch the wading birds spear fish with their beaks and diving birds that would pick fish up with their talons.

Jeanne was slow to walk because she was so unstable on her little feet. She fell and cried a lot. Aida would pick her up, kiss her, rub her sore knees and many times carry her to the rocker on the porch. There, she would hug her dear little girl and comfort her by rocking her until all the sobs had disappeared.

Being rocked by Aida was part of Jeanne's life. Before nap time and bedtime, she would cuddle-up in Aida's lap, suck her thumb and listen to Aida's deep voice hum negro spirituals from her church. When Jeanne's eyes were droopy, Aida would carefully lay her down in her little bed to sleep with her teddy bear. Afterwards, Aida always stayed for a quiet rest in the rocking chair, humming and rocking, humming, and rocking.

Sometimes, when Nell watched Jeanne learning to walk, saying a few words and changing quickly, she longed for Jeanne's half- sister Nell Leigh. It was time my little Nell Leigh joined our family, she thought as she gazed outside watching Aida help Jeanne walk down their brick sidewalk.

That evening, after Neal had finished his dinner, Nell suggested they take a stroll. "It's such a lovely evening. We never walk like we used to when you were courting me.'﹐

Neal looked at his wife, lit a cigar and smiled. "You want something, don't you?" He asked. "Let's walk to our gazebo and talk."

"Now, sugar, why would you think I want something? Can't I just want to stroll with my handsome husband?"

Neal didn't answer. He just puffed on his cigar as they made their way across the lawn to the gazebo. "Okay, what's on your mind?" He asked, stretching his legs out in front of him and putting his arm, loosely around Nell's shoulder.

"Isn't it lovely out, tonight? We should do this more often," Nell said, in an intimate voice she reserved for Neal.

Neal laughed, blew a couple of smoke rings in the air and asked, "Nell, sooner or later you're going to have to tell me what you want."

"Well, I've been watching Jeanne change from a baby to a little girl, and I think it would be nice if she knew her half-sister, Nell Leigh, before she's ready for college. It would be nice if the family is together. It doesn't seem right that the sisters are separated," Nell said, leaning over and giving Neal a small kiss on his cheek.

"Hmm," he said.

Nell could see his wheels turning as he sat there quietly smoking that smelly cigar.

"I suppose it makes sense to have Jeanne know her sister. I hadn't given Nell Leigh a thought, but for the sake of bringing the family together, I guess it's all right. How old is she anyway?

"She's eight. She was born less than a year after I was married to Winton."

"If you're sure Nell Leigh wants to live with us, call Moma Leigh and tell her we will pick up Nell on the weekend. I don't think she likes me, and I don't know how she feels about Jeanne," Neal stated, looking at his wife for her approval.

"Oh, sugar, thank you. I'll make all the arrangements. It will be wonderful to have our family all under one roof. We'll all be fine."

"I hope so, Nell. I hope so," Neal said, standing up and tossing his cigar butt into the grass. Let's go in," I want to read the paper."

A week later, Nell Leigh arrived, and Jeanne's life was changed forever. Jeanne idolized her older sister and tried to be with her, but Nell Leigh ignored her, rarely acknowledging her.

But Jeanne's innocent interest in her, and her own boredom and loneliness, caused Nell Leigh to spend small amounts of time with her. One hot summer's day when Jeanne was two and a half, Nell Leigh watched her from the porch, lying on her stomach, on the brick walk, looking at ants.

"Hi," Nell Leigh said. "Wanna take a walk around here with me?"

Jeanne smiled, said a couple of unintelligible words in agreement and toddled off after Nell Leigh.

When Aida looked out the window to check on Jeanne on her way to the kitchen, she saw her following Nell Leigh, way across the yard.

After a time, Aida went outside and started looking for Jeanne. Suddenly she saw Nell Leigh carrying Jeanne in her arms. She could hear Jeanne sputtering, coughing, and talking gibberish in her usual manner.

"What happened to Jeanne, Nell Leigh?" Aida asked, roughly, her dark eyes looking suspiciously at the girl.

Jeanne fell in the pond before I could do anything about it. "I saved her," Nell Leigh said, proudly. "Ugh, here take her. She's heavy and all wet."

"Are you sure that's what happened?"

"Absolutely," Nell Leigh announced and ran across the grass, up the stairs and into the house.

"Come on baby, Aida will get you all cleaned up," Aida said, cuddling her chubby little friend in her arms.

That night at dinner, Nell Leigh told her mother and stepfather her story of saving Jeanne's life embellishing it childishly.

Continual bickering between Nell and Neal developed after Nell Leigh moved in with them. Nell felt Neal didn't treat Nell Leigh as well as he did Jeanne.

"I don't agree, Nell," Neal said, one night after they had gone to their bedroom. "She lives here, eats our food, wears the clothes we provide, what more do you want?"

"I want you to love her the way you love Jeanne," Nell said, quietly in a venomous tone. "Nell, I'm trying to run a bank, keep all of you cared for, I can't do any more than that."

"Why won't you admit you don't love her because she's another man's child?"

Neal silently undressed, went into the bathroom to shower, came back and went to bed, not saying a word. After that, the hours he worked increased, and Nell accused him of becoming a workaholic.

The following spring, Jeanne was three and getting very adventurous. She also was speaking clearly and making herself understood. Aida would help her dress and let her go outside to explore the yard on her own, more and more.

Aida would watch her little charge from the window and occasionally, Jeanne would fall. Aida would run out as fast as she could to pick little Jeanne up, kiss her, and say, "Honey Child, I wish you could walk better in the grass. It seems so hard for you."

One morning, all dressed in a little seersucker sun suit and full of breakfast, Jeanne announced to Aida, "I go out to play, now," and she slid out of her highchair and pushed the screen door open.

"Don't you wander too far away, you hear," Aida warned her.

Jeanne was sliding down the front steps on her bottom by then. Standing m and balancing on her odd little feet, Jeanne started down the sidewalk. She stopped bent over and picked up something soft. "Aida, I found a birdie," she yelled.

Suddenly, she screamed, "Birdie bite me, ow, ow, go away birdie, birdie bite my head." She dropped the baby bird and limped quickly to the porch as the mother Blue Jay flew to baby on the sidewalk where Jeanne had dropped it.

The next day and days after that, every time she went out to play, she would announce to Aida, "Momma birdie not bite me," as she put her arms over her head when she opened the door.

That summer in the afternoons when Nell was entertaining, either one of her numerous bridge groups or her non-card playing society friends, she would instruct Aida to keep Jeanne away from the party. Aida would surprise Jeanne with a picnic lunch and an afternoon fishing and wading in a local pond. After lunch, Jeanne would cuddle in Aida's arms as Aida rested against a big, old tree and go to sleep. Slowly, Aida would lay down and together they would take a long nap in the shade with Aida's arms protecting her little treasure.

During the winter months, Aida and Jeanne spent afternoons exploring Lakeland by bus. They would get on at one end and ride to the other end, first. Then, they would repeat their ride, stopping at streets that had candy stores, ice cream parlors or movie theaters and get off there. Sometimes, Aida took Jeanne to a Disney movie and treated her to an ice cream cone, afterwards. When it was time to go home, they'd ride to an appointed stop and wait for Nell to come and drive them home.

With Aida as her constant companion, the first six years of Jeanne's life were secure. When her mother told her that Aida had gone, one day, Jeanne was heartbroken. Aida hadn't said goodbye to her, and Jeanne's source of love and kindness had suddenly dried up.

Added to the loss of Aida, her mother announced the family was moving to Orlando. Everyone and everything had changed overnight. The very day Jeanne turned six, the moving van arrived to take all their belongings to their new home. She sat on the front porch watching the men go in and out of her house, carrying everything and putting it in the truck.

"Dad, where are they taking all our things?" she asked.

"They are taking them to our new home. Stay here on the porch and soon we'll go in the car to our home, too."

"But Dad, I want to stay here!"

"Nonsense, you'll love Orlando."

Minutes later, he put her in the back seat of the car and said, "Don't move. We'll be going soon."

Her mother came out carrying her cake, put it firmly in her lap and said, "Don't let go of it. I don't want cake all over the car.',

Jeanne whispered, "I want Aida. Where are you, Aida?"

"What's that, Jeanne?" Her handsome father asked, all smiles.

"Nothing, Father," she said, taking the back of hand and wiping her eyes.

"That's my good little girl," he replied.

If there is something we wish to change in a child, we should examine it and see whether it is something that could better be changed in ourselves. Carl Jung

2. A YOUNG REBEL

1940 - 1950

JEANNE

On September 7th, 1940, Hitler began his Blitzkrieg – his lightning war against Great Britain. Hitler's nightly bombing raids were destroying factories and killing people all over England. War fever had been ignited in America and the nation was gearing up in a lend-lease program, producing the goods that Britain needed to fight Germany.

At the same time, Neal, beyond the age of the draft, was the president of a bank in Orlando, Florida.

Being president was a big job for Neal and he traveled a great deal. Many years later, it was hinted that his expertise in finance had been called upon in Washington D.C. for the war effort. Many nights, Nell, Nell Leigh and Jeanne dined alone.

Jeanne often asked, "Mother, when is father coming home? I miss him."

"Your father is very busy being president of the bank and I will be traveling with him, in a week or so. He travels more since the war."

"I don't care whether he's here or not," Nell Leigh stated.

Quickly changing the subject when her mother gave her a criticizing look, she asked, "May I work on the school newspaper? I have plenty of time. All my subjects are so easy. I thought they would be much harder, but they aren't."

Of course, with your writing ability, they need someone like you to make that rag into a real newspaper.

"I plan on becoming the editor when I'm a sophomore," Nell Leigh replied confidently.

Nell gave her an approving smile. Turning to Jeanne she asked, "How are you doing, young lady? Do you like first grade?"

Ignoring her mother's questions, Jeanne asked, "Will Auntie May and Grandmother Greenfield come to take care of us, like they always do?"

"Yes, Jeanne," her mother said sounding exasperated. "I asked you a question? "How is school?"

"It's okay. I really like recess and gym the best." I'm not telling mother about the endless hours the teacher makes me spend in the cloakroom, Jeanne decided. I think it's because I talk too much.

"I hate the cafeteria ladies. They say I must stay until I drink my milk, but I won 't. I won't drink that nasty milk, even if I must stay there all day. I'm never in the class. I don 't know what they are doing in there" Jeanne thought.

"Jeanne, are you listening to me? You must stop that incessant daydreaming. Young southern ladies must always stay focused and work hard. You want 'A's like your sister.,,

"What does the maid have for dessert?" Jeanne asked.

"Oh, Jeanne, you're impossible, sometimes," Nell said, giving her youngest daughter a very impatient look.

Mother's mad at me and I don't know why. I don't know what 'A's ' are, but my mother and Nell Leigh know. She looked at her mother and asked, "When is father coming home?"

"We're going to meet his train, tomorrow afternoon. I wish the Orlando station wasn't so over-run with people. A lot of them look dirty."

"I like it. It's fun to watch all the people," Jeanne

retorted.

"Ugh, sometimes, Jeanne," her mother replied, folding her napkin and carefully putting it in its holder. "Sit up straight and don't take such big bites of your cake. Little southern ladies eat daintily," frowning at Jeanne.

Sitting there eating her cake, Jeanne thought, I can't wait to see Auntie May and

Grandmother Greenfield. They are so much fun, and we'll play cards. I love to play card games.

She smiled as she finished the last bite thinking about her card games but felt uncomfortable again when she glanced at her mother. She couldn't put it into words, but she never felt she could please her.

The next day, after school, Nell picked up Jeanne from school and drove to the train station. "Now, don't go wandering off. I'm going to see if your father's train is on time. I doubt it with all the soldiers on the trains, now days. We are certainly in the war.',

Her father's train was an hour late and Jeanne heard her mother blame it on the war. After Jeanne begged and begged for a candy bar, her mother relented and bought them both one for the long wait.

Jeanne heard the salesclerk at the newspaper stand say that she was having trouble getting chocolate bars and blamed it on the war. "Mother what is a war and why does it make father's train late and eat our chocolate bars?"

Her mother smiled for the first time that day and said, "More people are eating the candy bars, especially the soldiers. The war is a bad thing, but it doesn't eat chocolate bars. Now, eat your candy and ask no more questions. Mother has a headache with all these people milling around."

The sweet bar made Jeanne thirsty. Knowing better than to bother her mother, sitting there with her eyes closed, Jeanne went over to the bubbler and waited. Soon, a soldier came up, took a drink, looked at her and asked, "Do you want a drink, little girl?"

She nodded too shy to talk. He picked her up and held her while she sucked in the water. Was I thirsty, she thought as she smiled at the nice man when he put her down. Hobbling as fast as her sore little feet would take her, she sat down next to her mother. Her mother had never missed her.

A few minutes later, the station master's booming voice came over the PA system and said, "Train from Atlanta, Georgia is arriving in eight minutes. Let the passengers off before you try to board. There's plenty of time."

His voice awakened Nell and together, they stood and waited for Neal to come through the doors. When he appeared, he looked different to Jeanne. He smiled a tired smile when he saw them and twisted his way through the throngs of soldiers to them. As they pushed their way to the car, he said, "It's good to be home. The country is in a panic with the war."

Her dear father had mentioned that war, too. It must be an awful thing to eat her chocolate bars and make the country unhappy.

Two days later, when Jeanne woke up, she couldn't get out of bed. Her legs wouldn't work. She couldn't talk, was hot and suddenly felt a sudden gush of hot liquid spewing out of her. Over and over, it came out until there was nothing more. She felt sticky, hated the smell and the stuff all over her pajamas. When Nell came in to help her get dressed for school, she screamed.

Jeanne didn't remember anything else for days except for vaguely remembering having some man give her some awful medicine and someone else washing her with cool water, over and over and offering her drinks of water through a straw. At last, one morning, she opened her eyes and felt better.

"What happened to me?" she asked her Aunt Wisie.

"Gracious, child, you've been so sick, your mama called me and your other aunts to come and help her nurse you. We've been here for days, trying to help you recover from something called amoebic dysentery. Your mother said you must have gotten it at the train station. There are lots of soldiers who have it from the war and they gave it to you.',

"That war is a bad thing. It eats chocolate, makes the country unhappy and makes soldiers sick."

"Don't talk nonsense, child," she said, feeling Jeanne's forehead. "You're cool. Do you feel like getting up and eating?"

"I'm starving," Jeanne said, happily. When she got out of bed, her legs went all wobbly and she sat back down on the bed. Aunt Wisie helped her get dressed and together they went downstairs to the dining room where some of her aunts and her mother were all gathered drinking coffee and eating breakfast. After saying all kinds of silly things like they thought she was going to die and they were so tired of taking care of her, they said it was time to take her medicine.

Somehow, what they said made Jeanne feel to blame for getting sick.

"Here, Jeanne eat your cereal, it will make you feel better."

Jeanne looked at the bowl full of grits and gagged. "I want some toast and lots of jelly." "For heaven's sake, you are so fussy!" Aunt Wisie said, but she gave her what she wanted, anyway.

"Now, Jeanne, you must open your mouth and take your medicine. The doctor said so." "I won't unless you give me a dollar."

"A dollar? You can have a shiny, dime, that's all. Here, take it and open your mouth.

Once, she took her medicine, she heard several whispered

comments about how sick she got after the doctor gave her sulfur and she almost died. When they had thoroughly exhausted that subject, they went back to their gossiping, totally ignoring her. They would lower their voices, nod their heads in a disapproving manner and Jeanne knew someone had done something terrible.

They had a way of making Jeanne feel like an outcast. It was at those times, she missed Aida terribly.

One afternoon, her father, came home early, all smiles, surprising her. Where's your mother?

"I think she's upstairs," Jeanne answered, watching her father take the stairs two at a time.

That night at dinner, her father announced they were moving to Dade City wherever that was and live in the middle of a citrus grove.

"What's a citrus grove?" Jeanne asked.

"It's where there are hundreds of trees growing oranges, lemons and grapefruit," her father answered. "Wait 'till you smell their flowers. They are like the nicest perfume in the world."

"Do I hafta go to school there?"

"Of course, Jeanne," her mother interrupted, visibly upset with her question.

For the next few days, her father stayed home and smiled a lot. Then, the movers came again, took their furniture away and they drove to their new home in the middle of a citrus grove, like her father said.

He became much angrier after the move and came home earlier more often from his work than ever before. It made Jeanne nervous, but he enjoyed an occasional walk with her father and her around their citrus grove. Jeanne loved those times being able to be with him and talk to him when he was calm. He named the various kinds of fruit they were growing and taught her how to pluck an orange from the tree, so it didn't hurt the tree or the orange. She thought, as they were walking, my dad is so smart. I like being with him outdoors, but not at the dinner table.

One day, he took them to a new area where there was a herd of Brahma cattle grazing across the field.

The minute she saw them she yelled, "Look at them, they are beautiful"!

The cattle heard her, threw their heads around with wild eyes, startled and the next thing she knew, they began running right at her and her parents, snorting and making strange noises. Her father threw her and himself to the ground, told her mother to lie down, too, and they all lay in the tall grass hiding from the cattle.

"Shssh," he said softly. "Don't make a sound and don't move."

Seeing nothing to charge, the Brahmas veered away from the flimsy fence and ran in another direction until they got tired, stopped and started grazing again.

When they walked back, her father was noticeably quiet, and it was the last time he took her on a walk near the cattle.

Occasionally, her mother would take her with her to her father's office. It wasn't a bank; it was a big building. Jeanne sounded out the big words written on the side of the building, Pasco Packing Company. Outside, she saw truckloads of oranges parked near the building.

Inside she saw, "Mr. Greenfield" written on the door of a big room. She thought, he's very important. Her father and mother took her with them on a walk through the big double doors to the plant and there her father explained how they made citrus juice from the oranges she had seen outside. The room was noisy, the equipment shiny and a lot of young men were working there. Her father explained they were German prisoners of war who were here to help make juice.

She liked the men. They always smiled at her and a spoke

a few words to her in German and English.

Third grade in Dade City had started several weeks before she came. She hated being the new kid and not starting with the rest of the kids. When her teacher introduced her to the class, she immediately noticed several of the girls passing notes back and forth, looking at her and giggling. The boys, on the other hand, smiled at her in a friendly way and even talked to her.

Jeanne didn't understand why the girls weren't friendly. Led by one girl, named Hazel, she was alternately taunted and ignored, making her life hell for the two years she attended the Dade City Schools.

She had suffered emotionally and physically because of her family's nomadic lifestyle. On average her tender roots were periodically yanked-up every one and half to two years or so and she was plunked down in a new school.

One day a new boy appeared in her class. He was friendly and became her best friend. His name was Gerald Claire Hutchinson. He liked to be called Claire. Each day after school, they played together, told each other stories about their families and Jeanne was happy to have found a friend. They remained constant companions from third to fifth grade until Jeanne moved away after fifth grade. Memories of him were etched in her mind and tucked away in her heart.

In fourth grade, instead of being the teacher's pet, she became the teacher's nemesis.

Punished during school for small infractions of her teacher's strict rules and banished to the cloak room was an everyday occurrence. The same thing happened at home, only it was her bedroom, for violating mother's strict rules of etiquette. Jeanne never accepted the rules and the punishment continued at school and home throughout the third, fourth and fifth grade.

Early on, Jeanne developed a way of coping with her

banishment at home by closing her door and crawling under her trundle bed. Hidden from the world by the long bedspread enclosing her, with just enough room left by the missing trundle, she felt safer. Under there, she would light a candle. The light from the candle was a beacon to help her find and talk to Spirit.

"Spirit, I am so lonely. I have been punished all day at school and now by my mother. I don't know what I'm doing wrong. I want to go home and be with you."

She always started out feeling angry, betrayed, and lonely. As she calmed down and talked to Spirit, her emotions changed, and she felt relief and finally a loving presence.

A bright spot in her world were her ballet and tap lessons she took in town. Even though her feet hurt her continually, she loved her dance lessons. Every spring when her mother drove her to her big performance in the classes' big extravaganza, Jeanne could feel her mother's irritation, but Nell did it, even though it meant missing a bridge game or social tea.

Occasionally, Nell Leigh came home to visit from boarding school and later on, college. Her mother invariably planned on Nell Leigh taking Jeanne along with her wherever she went so Nell could maintain her social schedule.

Nell Leigh grumbled about having to do it and made Jeanne sit in the rumble seat of the car when they went anywhere, as far from her as possible. Nell Leigh's ability to drive was reasonable unlike her mother's, but one afternoon, Jeanne felt uneasy when she climbed into the back. She didn't dare say a word to her crabby sister because she knew Nell Leigh didn't want to take her. That day Nell took a short cut and their car got stuck in the mud and was in a dangerous slant. It scared Jeanne terribly and she started to cry.

"Stop crying Jeanne, we're alright. Come on. We must walk to that farmhouse. They will help us," yanking Jeanne's hand. "I don't know why you are carrying on so, you big baby."

Two things happened in Dade City Schools; she became the teacher's pet and made herself sick looking for attention from her mother. She ended up with bronchitis almost once a month that year but didn't get her heart's desire. Her mother hired a nurse to take care of her.

Jeanne hated being put in an oxygen tent each time to help her breathe. The overpowering odor of the medicine in there made her sick. She constantly tested the rules and stuck her nose out of the tent whenever the nurse wasn't looking. She desperately didn't want to be in there.

It was there that Jeanne began to learn how to read people's actions, their expressions and body language and know almost what they were thinking. She became very alert to any signs when the girls were planning some prank to play on her and prepared herself before it even happened. When they did whatever their little naughty minds had devised, she would be ready for them and leave without a word when it was over. It was the way she survived.

Added to her trouble with the girls, Jeanne found that her old school in Orlando was on a different educational schedule than Dade City Schools. It meant that Jeanne missed a lot of the basics including cursive handwriting and reading using phonic skills to attack the words

But Jeanne was a survivor and very intelligent. She taught herself to write by watching the teacher write on the board. However, learning to read well was a different matter and English became her most difficult subject.

"I don't know, either," Jeanne sobbed, "but I just get all scared inside when I'm in a car and it is on a slant, like today." The mystery of her unusual fear would be solved, but not until much later in Jeanne's life.

It had become very obvious to Jeanne as she grew older, how little time Nell wanted to spend with her youngest daughter. Jeanne accepted her mother's attitude, stoically. She had only Aida, her loving negro nanny, to compare her mother to and Aida had become a distant memory.

She realized that her mother's world did not include her, and she didn't like her mother's friends, anyway. They all seemed so phony to her. Sometimes, she would listen to her mother play the part of the beautiful, charming, southern lady. Jeanne would hear her mother continually remind her friends of her aristocratic background and wealthy family through her clever stories at her never-ending bridge parties and social gatherings. One of her favorite stories was about her very lovely childhood as the baby of her very wealthy family, adored by everyone.

Her heritage was so much a part of her strong personality, when she talked about Henry Lee, a brave officer in the 'War between the States,' she would become very emotional. She extolled his accomplishments and claimed he was a distant relative to her family. In later years, Nell established an alumni organization for all of his descendants and spearheaded a reunion with them every year.

The other subject that made Nell very angry was her hatred of the Yankees who she claimed ruined the south. Her wide circle of friends was quick to agree with Nell and flatter her ego to remain on her invitation list.

Usually, Jeanne was able to escape her mother's punishment on the days her mother was entertaining because her mother's attention was concerned with reciting the same stories over and over of how many men wanted to marry her because of her beauty. She also weaved her aristocratic, wealthy background, into the stories she told, always ending with her great debut as Beauty Queen of Gasparilla, Florida.

Glossing over her first unsuccessful marriage to her alcoholic husband, she quickly described Jeanne's father as a brilliant, very successful president or vice president of whatever business or bank was lucky enough to have him.

Many days Jeanne would lie down in her hammock, away from the loud voices of her mother's friends and look up at the sky. Up there she'd watch the sun's rays coming through the clouds and pretend that she was walking up through the clouds and leaving the Earth. All through her life, clouds fascinated her and connected her to God and the Holy Spirit.

In their citrus grove, Jeanne had another favorite hiding spot. It was a special tangerine tree that she loved to climb. The tree's branches fanned out from the main tree and formed a small, wide place where Jeanne loved to perch. Up there, she would talk to Spirit, sometimes asking to be taken to heaven after an especially hurtful day of being bullied.

Jeanne had a dog she loved named Dandy who waited for her every day after school. He would run and greet her, wagging his tail, running round and round her, wild to see her. He was a big, black mutt that had appeared on their doorstep one day, hungry. Jeanne took pity on him, fed him some scraps and from then on they were friends. Each afternoon, she would walk all through the orange groves with him after school, telling him her troubles.

One day, a big, rumbling truck arrived with a lot of noise coming from the back. The truck drove down the road on their property and stopped. She and Dandy followed and when the farmer opened the back and turkeys came out, Dandy started to bark and chase them. The farmer shook his head and said, "That there, dog is a-go'in to run those turkeys off, if' n you don't stop him." Your father bought them. Dandy chased those turkeys all over the property and finally chased them away. When her father learned that they were missing, Dandy didn't meet her after school that afternoon. Jeanne called and called, but he never came. After searching everywhere for him, Jeanne knew something had happened to him. Maybe he had been hit by a farm truck. She was heartbroken because she loved Dandy, her only friend. Later, she learned that her father had taken him away. Knowing that her father wouldn't ever tell her what he had done, Jeanne was heartbroken. Dandy was gone and she would never see him again.

She experienced the same kind of pain when she watched families going to church with their children who ganged up on her and bullied her in school. She couldn't understand how they could love God and torment her so much. She decided they pretended to be good people, but really weren't. They were phonies.

In December, right after Christmas, her father said during dinner that they were moving to Jacksonville, Florida. Jeanne was stunned by his announcement. She was just feeling like she belonged, and they were moving again, to another new school, more new kids and a different teacher. Jeanne fell sick to her stomach as she thought about the move.

Jeanne was filled with dread being the new girl entering school in January, the middle of the school year. The teacher took an instant dislike to her and embarrassed her terribly by sending her out to the cloakroom at every opportunity. Jeanne secretly knew why it happened most of the time. Sonny Merada played a big part in her banishment. He liked her and would make faces at her while she was attempting to give a talk in front of the class. She would laugh and giggle. There was a part of her that loved to rebel against authority. She couldn't do it at home, but she could at school. The result was she caused the teacher to be angry and the effect on her was to spend time in the cloakroom.

Although, academically challenged, Jeanne was becoming a real beauty. She attracted the boys to her like bees to honey. Being beautiful was both an asset and a liability. The boys loved her and the little princesses were jealous of her. Diane Ballard, the daughter of Nell's best friend, was a member of the royalty. Jeanne's looks and her magnetism with the boys was a definite threat to Diane. She became obsessed with Jeanne and challenged her continually by spearheading a campaign with her group to spread lies and ugly rumors about Jeanne.

In sixth grade, Sonny was sent to a private, military day school and he saw Jeanne every chance he could. She became his girlfriend but didn't limit her boyfriends to just Sonny.

Boys found her at parties and dances, a social necessity to the sixth grade kids. Their hormones were just beginning to make the opposite sex much more interesting. It was at their parties, they had physical contact with each other in an approved manner. Overwhelmed with each other, at a dance or social gathering, boys asked girls to go steady, stole a kiss or two and began their search for a perfect mate.

Afterwards, filled with bravado, boys' locker room conversations dwelt on their dancing partners' figures in great detail producing loud outbursts of raucous laughter. But in the girl's bedrooms after school, the whispered conversations were more about how well certain boys danced, who was handsome and who was fun to be with.

Because her mother usually wasn't pleased with the friends and their families that Jeanne liked, she insisted that Jeanne's father take a more active role to save Jeanne from her innocent social engagements by appearing in the early evening and bringing her home from the affair. On one particular evening, she was terribly embarrassed by him when he showed up at the Patrol Dance and escorted her home before the dance had hardly begun. The parents of the boy she was going with had picked her up, taken her to the dance, chaperoned the dance and were going to bring her home, but didn't have the chance. Jeanne was sure that that little story was laughed about the next day in her class and the boy's parents thought her father's behavior was ridiculous.

Jeanne continued with her favorite out-of- school activity, her dance classes in tap and ballet. She was terribly disappointed when the ballet teacher said her feet and toes couldn't bear the weight of her body. She was not allowed to go up on her toes like all the other girls. Feeling different and alone was a familiar pattern for Jeanne, one she didn't like and even happened in dance class.

Sonny kept in touch with Jeanne throughout the year and in the spring, he asked if she could be his date for military day at his school. He and she would be at the head of the troop and walk under crossed swords and open a dance, together. She was thrilled with the whole idea. It seemed so romantic.

As summer approached, her mother began taking her on little shopping trips, buying her lots of sport clothes. When Jeanne asked her why, Nell replied, "You are going to camp for the summer."

"If I go anywhere, I want to go to Keystone with my friends," Jeanne said, bravely.

"You will go to Skyland because that's where Nell Leigh went, and she liked it."

Her mother stated her decision as a fact. There was no discussion about it. Jeanne bridled with fury. She was told what to do and never given the chance to plead her case. It had always been that way.

Jeanne overheard her mother talking to her friend about how happy she would be having Jeanne out of her hair for two months so she could travel with her husband, attend parties without having to worry what Jeanne was up to and have the freedom of not having to deal with her.

For Jeanne, although disappointed not to be going with her friends, she looked forward to getting out from under her mother's social rules. If she had to listen to another lecture on what southern young ladies of good standing were supposed to do, she'd scream.

But like all children who had never been away from home before, camp life suddenly became lonely, and Jeanne wanted to go home. Her young counselor was very nice and smiled sweetly at Jeanne, but said, "No, Jeanne, your parents signed you up for two months and two months it will be unless you get sick or injured."

I'll get home, she thought as she left. I'll think of something.

That afternoon, Jeanne had devised her plan. She took a walk in the woods looking for the plant she needed to carry out her escape. "Ah, there you are," she said to the group of poison ivy plants growing quietly in the shade of the forest. Reaching down, she picked a bunch of them, looked around, furtively, and stuffed them into her underpants beneath her shorts. Walking back to camp nonchalantly with a pant full of the noxious weed, she opened the door of her cabin and at that moment, felt the burning.

What have I done? I feel like I am on fire! I didn't think I'd feel so terrible, she thought and raced for the outdoor bathrooms to wash the awful stuff away in the shower. She washed her body with soap, but it didn't take away the itching and burning. She watched as her skin made huge bubbles filled with liquid which broke when she scratched her skin.

She wrapped herself in a towel and ran for her counselor. She took one look at Jeanne and took her to the small dispensary where the nurse just nodded and asked her what she had been doing lying down in patches of poison ivy. Jeanne pretended she didn't hear her and began screaming that she was burning. The nurse quickly began covering her with calamine lotion.

Two weeks later, Jeanne had fully recovered, but had not been successful in her childish attempt to be sent home, she was sent to her grandmother's home, instead. Jeanne found that Moma Leigh had more rules than her mother. She spent the rest of the summer at her grandmother's.

Her grandmother was becoming senile and demanded that Jeanne wear winter clothing in the middle of the summer so she wouldn't get cold. The temperature hovered around 95 degrees and Jeanne would hide and take off her sweaters every chance she could.

Looking back, Jeanne equated her punishment from the Universal Law of cause and effect, again. She caused her internment at her grandmother's and the effect was a summer of living with grandmother's copious senile rules. It was a pattern that followed Jeanne.

During camp the next summer, Jeanne wanted to swim on the swim team. The two near drowning episodes when she was six and seven were distant memories. She was ready for a summer in the water. She innocently signed up for the swim meet believing she could participate, but taken aside by the swimming coach and told, "Jeanne, you aren't ready to swim in the meet."

"Why not?" Jeanne asked, defensively.

"Your strokes aren't good enough, yet. Maybe, later on, but not now."

Her words stung and made Jeanne all the more determined to be in future meets. Jeanne was a survivor and she also was a fighter. When she wanted something badly enough she would do everything she could think of to make it happen.

Every day, she would sit by the pool and watch the girl who was the best swimmer in camp, swim the crawl. She would observe every minute detail of the girl's swimming ability. Then she would get in the water and practice what she had just seen. Teaching herself by observing others was an integral pattern in Jeanne's personality, something she would do throughout her life. That summer, she taught herself to swim so well she won first place in many of the swim meets.

Bored one night at their campfire sing, Jeanne whispered to her cohorts, "Why don't we sneak out of camp tonight after hours and go find the Holy Rollers? I think they are near Clyde, North Carolina. Want some excitement? It'll be fun."

"Yah, let's go find the snake charmers," a friend

replied.

"I've always wanted to see them do that," Jeanne said. "I won't believe it until I see it." They walked fast and were at Clyde before they knew it.

When they were sneaking back into camp, a friend whispered "Do you believe it now?"

"I sure do. That Holy Roller Minister was like a magician making that old snake go into a trance weaving his ugly head back and forth. There was something scary and exciting about the whole thing. Do you all want to go again?"

Everyone whispered, "Yah," as they crept into their cabins.

All summer long and for several summers after that, Jeanne and her friends paid visits to many different revival meetings every chance they could. They were never caught, and the taste of rebellion fed Jeanne's adventurous spirit.

Back home after a summer at camp, tanned and healthy from her summer sports, Jeanne started seventh grade. Jeanne sensed the teacher was not her friend. Although she was still challenged academically and Diane Ballard was still in her class, Jeanne had developed a group of friends and she was beginning to feel more at home in school.

Around Christmas time, one night at dinner, her mother said, brightly, in that irritating false manner she had of speaking when she had to say something that was difficult, "We are moving back to Dade City after Christmas. Isn't that wonderful?

Jeanne immediately thought, at least I know the school system and will escape Dianne. I wonder if father got a better position than before. I know I can't ask him. She and her father never talked about his work, but she learned from her mother after they moved that he had decided to build and established another fruit juice plant that specialized in making fruit concentrate.

Life was good for Jeanne when she walked happily back into her school and the seventh grade with its familiar surroundings. Arriving halfway through the year, she hoped she wasn't too far behind academically. Being able to survive would depend upon her teacher and what she expected of Jeanne. Sitting down in back, she saw many familiar faces, some old bullies and some friends.

"Good morning, class. I see a new face in the back. Welcome, my name is Mrs. Corcoran." She looked directly at Jeanne and smiled. "Hello, would you stand up and tell the class your name."

Jeanne liked her. Her voice was pleasant and she had given Jeanne a welcome that seemed very sincere. "My name is Jeanne Greenfield," she said, quietly and sat down. A cute girl in front of her turned around and whispered, quickly, "Hi, I'm Mary Alice, the teacher's daughter," she whispered. "Have lunch with me and I'll introduce you around."

Sitting there stunned and surprised, Jeanne thought, How lucky can I be? No girl has ever been so nice to me the first day. "I'd love to too, thanks," Jeanne said, giving Mary Alice a little smile.

Jeanne quickly learned that Mrs. Corcoran was a good teacher and a fair disciplinarian. The bullying was discouraged by her sharp eyes. She would intercept most of the notes being passed by a certain group of girls, throw them in the waste basket and mete out punishment by assigning extra math problems or essays on paying attention in class. After a while, that deterred a lot of the hate mail. But the under-current was still there.

Jeanne had a reasonably good year academically with her seasoned teacher who was able to explain things to Jeanne, clearly. The result was a better than average report card for Jeanne which she happily gave to her parents.

Being best friends with Mary Alice gave Jeanne a much-needed outlet for her enthusiasm, playfulness, and someone to talk to, girl to girl. She practically lived at Mary Alice's home and became friends with Mary Alice's three brothers, and one in particular named Michael. He was good looking and lots of fun. Mary Alice's family became her second family. All the silly rules of etiquette were never discussed by any of them. It was like a breath of fresh air being there.

Mary Alice's father, Francis, was a kind and loving man who Jeanne loved. He wasn't home a great deal because he traveled on business to Central and South America. He had a chicken factory in Cuba during Castro's beginning rise to power. In one day, he lost everything in Cuba when Castro's government came and took over his business without warning. All foreign private companies were confiscated. Communism was the law of the land.

But for Jeanne and Mary Alice, their lives were not changed. The two girls shared confidences about everything including boys, their families, the mean girls in their class, and on a higher note, religion. Jeanne admired Mary Alice because she was a real, spiritual friend who lived her religion. Jeanne had begun to have deep stirrings of spirituality inside her and she wanted to explore the various churches in town and what they stood for. It was made easy for her to do that by going with her friends.

After talking with Mary Alice about it, Jeanne was delighted when Mary Alice asked, "Would you like to go to Mass with me, Sunday?" My dad will be home and he'll take us.

"What does your father do?"

"I'm not quite sure, but my mother says he travels all over the world for his company. I love my dad."

It pleased her to know how nice Mary Alice's father was and Jeanne thought, Here 's my chance to see what the Mass is with my best friend. I hope my folks don 't find out, but if they do and have a fit that I went to a Catholic church, I don 't care. She giggled and said, "Sure, I'd love to go," feeling very rebellious. It was a glorious feeling.

She borrowed Mary Alice's catechism book to read a few days before they went to Mass. She tucked the book under her jacket when she got home from school and hid it under her bed before dinner that night. Racing upstairs after dinner, she crawled under her bed, lit a candle and proceeded to read. Her face began to frown as she read, and she finally closed the book with an irritated snap.

The next day at school, Mary Alice asked, "What did you think of the book?"

"To tell the truth, I didn't like all the rules you have to follow. The book doesn't explain why, it just says you are a sinner if you don't follow the rules and will go to hell!"

"That's what we are taught. I never really thought about it. I just do it. When I mess up, I go to confession and all my sins are wiped away."

Jeanne thought, I'll go with her because she's my best friend and it will bother my parents if they find out, but I'm not going to be a Catholic.

After Jeanne had gone to Mass the following Sunday, Nell got a call from one of her friends saying they saw Jeanne coming out of the Catholic Church when they were driving home from the Episcopalian service.

When Neal came home from the bank, that evening, Nell followed him up to their bedroom and said, "Our daughter was seen leaving the Catholic Church on Sunday. What are we going to do about it?"

"I can't believe our daughter. It's terrible. See that you do something about it."

A few days later, her mother said, more pleasantly than usual, "Next Sunday, I would like to go to church with you, Jeanne, and take you to my beautiful Episcopalian Church. It's more like a chapel, but I know you'll like it."

She must have found out about my visit to the Catholic Church. One of her friends saw me go in or come out, Jeanne thought. Understanding her mother's subtle method of steering Jeanne away from other churches, she agreed. At least her mother was actually going with her without her aunts or other adult friends. Nell was spending a little real time with her for a change.

When they arrived, Nell walked to the front of the church and chose the first pew. She turned and glanced imperiously around the church as if to say, I'm from a long line of southern aristocrats who came over here from England. She knew everyone was watching her as she sat down with a satisfied look on her face.

Leaving the service, Nell said, "Your father and I want you to be confirmed in the Episcopalian Church. As true southerners, we feel it is the only acceptable church for people in our social class to belong to. We don't go to the Catholic Church or the Jewish Synagogue.

Those are for people who don't have our heritage." Jeanne wanted to vomit listening to yet another lecture on how important lineage was to her mother.

"Most northerners don't understand us when they move down here. They think we should welcome them with open arms. Being able to trace our heritage back three and four generations is very important to us. It sets the social order in the south.

They also get all high and mighty about the way we treat our Negroes, but they don't understand what we know about our servants. They have been with us for generations and have certain characteristics. They are child-like and need to be cared for. We provide jobs for them that they are able to do, such as cleaning our houses and taking care of our small children. But they don't have the capabilities to go out and compete in the white man's world."

Jeanne couldn't believe the poppycock her mother was telling her. Her mother actually believed what she was saying. Jeanne had become like Aida's child and the things Aida taught her how to live and love. The discussions they had about everything were deeper than she had ever had with her mother or father.

But she liked the idea of her mother actually talking to her and not sending her to her room for some infraction of the rules Nell lived by. However, it made her blood run cold listening to the bigoted attitude her mother had about other religious denominations and all Negroes.

They rode home in silence and Jeanne learned more about her mother that day than she wanted to know.

That night at dinner, Nell went on and on about the lovely day she had had with Jeanne and asked, "Jeanne, did you like the church services, today?"

"I did, but I still want to explore more before I am confirmed."

"Honestly, Jeanne, after I spent the entire morning with you, you can be so exasperating!" her mother snapped back.

"I have a right to think for myself. I'm not rubber stamp material," Jeanne replied folding her arms over her chest and clenching her jaw.

She saw her mother's face go red and tight, and she said in a cold and angry way, "You are not to leave your room, except to go to school for the next week, you rude and unappreciative girl."

Jeanne didn't say a word, she knew better, but she thought, I want to yell at her, but if I do, I'll be in my room, forever. I will bide my time. I don 't care. It's my life and I'm going to find out where I belong.

By the time her banishment was over, Jeanne had spent many hours reading and thinking about churches. She was ready to explore another church. She asked the King twins, good friends of hers, to take her to their Baptist Church on Sunday. She told her mother she was invited to stay Saturday night with her friend, Mary Alice.

"I wish you would spend more time with some of my friends' daughters. I don't like you only seeing Catholics. And I don't want you to go to church with her again," Her mother said, crisply. If you do, you will find yourself in your room for a month!"

Jeanne glanced at her mother and thought, mother would burst if she knew where I'm really going this Sunday.

She stayed with Mary Alice but met the King girls on the corner just as they had planned and walked quickly to their church in the next block. Jeanne prayed that none of her mother's friends were driving by as she ran up the stairs of the church. Inside, Jeanne whispered, "Let's sit in the back."

Sitting down, together, Evelyn whispered, "Our minister is having an affair with a woman in town," and giggled.

"Are you sure?" Jeanne whispered back, her eyes dancing with mischief. "I can see why, he's handsome."

Elizabeth giggled and added, "I think so, too."

The organ mistress had started to play, and Jeanne settled back ready to absorb everything about the church. She sang their hymns, put money in the collection plate and waited expectantly for the handsome minister to give the sermon.

At first, his tone of voice was soft and appealing, but as he went on, it began to rise with anger. Jeanne felt like he was hurling thunderbolts of rage at them. As his ugly words began to spew out of his mouth in a thunderous voice about eternal damnation, over and over, Jeanne tuned him out. She was a master at that. She had been doing it with her mother for years.

Afterwards, as they were filing out, Jeanne thought, Thank God that's over. He might be handsome, but what I heard makes me feel awful. How could a loving God think or act like this to all of us down here on Earth? Church isn't supposed to make me feel like this. It's supposed to make me feel good. I'll never be a Baptist.

"Did you like our minister?" Evelyn and Elizabeth asked almost in unison.

"He's too loud for me," Jeanne replied, not wanting to lose their friendship.

The following week she told her mother she was invited to stay overnight with Mary Alice again.

"Honestly, Jeanne, you are spending far too much time with Mary Alice. Be sure you don't go to church with her!" Her mother's scornful look was all Jeanne needed to encourage her to go.

During the week, Jeanne had arranged to meet Cousin Meredith at the Methodist Church on Sunday. She liked the interior of the building, but not the sermon. After the service, Meredith asked her how she liked the service and Jeanne replied, "I think it was nice, but not for me. Secretly, she thought, the minister's voice wasn't as loud, but his message was just as mean as the Baptist minister. I'm not going there again.

The rest of seventh grade went well for Jeanne. She went to parties and dances, saw more of Gerald Clair than her parents liked and suffered the insults of the bully girls with resistance and resignation. She never openly confronted them; she just ignored them.

In eighth grade, her teacher was inexperienced and unable to keep control of the high-spirited young pre-teens. Jeanne tested the teacher's patience and ended up writing the Preamble to the Constitution 100 times as punishment. Her grades were passing, and Jeanne didn't worry about them. She was having too much fun, socially with her friends and Gerald Claire.

Her father gave her a car to drive to and from school. She

didn't have a license, but none of the kids did. It was a farming community and children were driving around their farms and into town as soon as they could see over the dashboard and reach the pedals. The local police knew everyone and turned a blind eye to the youngsters behind the wheel.

An added bonus of having her own car was the freedom it brought her. She could see her old friend, Claire, anytime she wanted. She pretended she didn't feel anything special when she was around him, but their relationship was deepening. They found a special song that they love to dance to: "Always." It expressed the puppy love that they felt for each other.

On Saturdays, they would meet at the movies and spend the afternoons together in the darkened theater. It was a wonderful time for both of them. They shared the innocent intimacy of two young people experiencing their first love. Sitting close together, being thrilled with each other, the wild adventures on the screen, and eating popcorn was nirvana. But like all human beings, they wanted to know more about each other.

Parties were the answer. Being a group of eager, inventive youngsters, a social group naturally developed. To spend more time together, they planned weekend parties in homes providing an intimacy that was impossible in a school setting. Their parents liked the idea of having the young people in their homes where they could keep an eye on them.

It was at one of those parties that Gerald Claire gave Jeanne her first kiss playing "Turtle."

The memorable power of that kiss would rest quietly in their hearts for nearly half a century before its full effects would be felt. That spring when Gerald' family moved to Tennessee, Jeanne felt a loss, sure that no one would ever replace him.

Like a good, aristocratic southern father, Neal Greenfield developed a sudden interest in Jeanne and what boy she was seeing in Dade City. He seemed obsessed, probably because her mother hated the class of people who lived there. He would appear, sporadically, at movies, dances and social gatherings, find Jeanne and take her home, leaving her partner to either find another date or go home. His clumsy attempts to keep his daughter unsullied by the boys made Jeanne all the more rebellious.

She wanted to find out why he was taking such an interest in her, something he had never done before. He had caused her a lot of embarrassment and that ugly feeling made her brave.

"Dad, why don't you want me to see my friends? They are fun and we aren't doing anything wrong."

"Your mother feels that our lineage makes us different from the local families in Dade City. We can trace our ancestors back into English history. The Earl of Talbot is a direct descendant on my father's side and your mother's family is descended from the illustrious Edward's Family. Your mother feels we have a position to maintain socially with our background. They came to this country, were given large land holdings in the south by the King of England and established a social order that came directly from centuries of English law. Over here, we have established a southern culture that we are proud of and want to maintain. I hope you remember your background and act accordingly. I like you to attend parties and dances. Just don't go with any particular boy."

It was the first and only time her father talked about the strata in southern culture and it saddened Jeanne to know that he didn't want her to see Claire, anymore.

When school ended, Nell surprised Jeanne by encouraging her to have a slumber party, inviting all her friends from Jacksonville. Thrilled by her mother's thoughtfulness, Jeanne did, but included Dade City friends, too. The party was a huge success and included Mary Alice's three brothers and boys from St. Leo's. Thoughts of Gerald receded as Jeanne threw herself into the preparations and actual party.

The boys performed to their audience of giggling girls. They were funny, cute and big show-offs. They noticed the girls and the girls made sure the boys noticed them, too, only in a more genteel, southern manner.

Michael was a constant in her life, because of being Mary Alice's brother and always around at home when she was there. He was like a brother in a lot of ways to her, but she also noticed his good looks.

Jeanne's parents began traveling more and more for business and some pleasure. Her father was a very intelligent man who used his charm and business sense to make his way up the ladder of success in the banking world. It was something he knew his wife required of him. Throughout his life, Neal had made strategic moves to further his career. Before every move they made, Neal's position was secure as either president or vice president. Before Neal retired, he had reaped huge financial rewards, satisfied his strong, demanding ego, and earned his wife's approval.

To assuage her guilt for leaving Jeanne, her mother confessed that she needed to be by her husband's side to protect the marriage. Jeanne didn't quite know what her mother meant at the time, but learned later that her handsome, worldly father had one affair during his marriage with his secretary but had never been tempted to leave his wealthy wife.

It was a relief for Jeanne when they were away. Older

now, she looked forward to all the secret parties she had when her parents were away. Everyone danced, hugged and sometimes kissed at those parties. In her social group, it was all the kids could think about and Jeanne's rebellious spirit was satisfied.

She also loved not having to worry about what rule of etiquette she had broken and being banished to her room. Her painful memories of being punished for some childish mistake or a remark her mother didn't like, haunted her. Thinking back, Jeanne remembered her mother heaping humiliation on her when she was a little defenseless child in such subtle ways that Jeanne felt powerless to fight back. She wanted to reach out and hit her mother but was too afraid to do that.

A bonus for Jeanne when home alone with her maid, was not being subjected to dinner table friction with her parents. The friction was so strong, sometimes, she felt it could have been like a match to start a fire. For whatever adult problems they were having with each other or with the outside world, it was always the time her father showed his anger and her mother focused on Jeanne and her inabilities to measure up to the family standards. Her father never interfered; he was just continually unpleasant to her at dinner. As soon as she could escape the dinner table, she would go to the living room piano and play, "Don't Fence Me In," as loudly as she could, over and over. Her mother usually appeared at the door and said, "That's enough, Jeanne. Find something else to do."

All the tension caused Jeanne to become a picky eater, although she was oblivious of that when she was young. With her parents away, Jeanne's appetite improved, and she enjoyed her meals of hot dogs and spaghetti, usually in the kitchen with the maid.

Her half-sister, Nell Leigh who was seven years older than Jeanne was always the perfect child in her mother's eyes. Nell Leigh had a photographic memory, was at the top of her class throughout high school, graduated with honors and was away at college when Jeanne was in grade school. She was so smart she tried out for the Vox Pop Quiz Show, went on the show, won, and was awarded a set of luggage, a trip and a date with a well-known radio host.

The spring of Jeanne's eighth grade year, Nell Leigh and De Car Worthington The Third were married. They had a huge wedding, 13 bride groomsmen, 13 bridesmaids. It was a beautiful affair that lasted six months. De Car was an angry, young man who showed it by beating Nell Leigh. Being a strong-willed young lady, she left and divorced him.

In the summer before Jeanne's freshman year, her family moved to Howie-in-the-Hills and Jeanne was again in a new school setting. It was a disaster for Jeanne academically and socially. Over Christmas vacation, they left and moved back to Dade City and Jeanne spent the last half of ninth grade in the Pasco High School System. She always wondered if her father had taken pity on her and decided to return to Dade City where Jeanne had been successful in school. Neither he nor her mother ever said, but Jeanne always wondered.

When Jeanne returned, she sought out the young Episcopal priest to learn more about his church and their belief system. Bursting with excitement, after she had left the priest, she rushed to see Mary Alice, to share her decision to be confirmed.

"Besides, the fact he's cute, he really took the time to explain what he believes the church stands for. He went into great depth about it, not just giving me a quick explanation. He also answered questions I have had all my life. My parents are Episcopalians, but they don't seem to understand what the church really stands for."

"I'm so happy you have decided. It will give you some peace in your life, I hope. I wish you wanted to be a Catholic, but being an Episcopalian is almost the same," Mary Alice replied, with a big smile on her face. At that moment, Jeanne loved Mary Alice so much for understanding her. Mary Alice was truly happy for her and later felt that Mary Alice was one of the most spiritual people she had ever known.

"But guess what? The best part is that I don't have to go to confession. I convinced him of my sincerity, and he dropped that part."

Jeanne's tone of voice dropped as she added. I'm sorry, Mary Alice, but I've seen your brothers go to confession and then go out and do the same thing all over again. They never learn. I think confession is ridiculous. I told the priest I have a straight phone line to God and don't need an intermediary. I'm sure that part of him doesn't believe in confession either."

When Jeanne told her parents of her decision to be confirmed in the Episcopal Church, they were pleased. For Jeanne, a spiritual yearning inside her had been satisfied for the time being.

The following fall, without consulting her, her parents announced that she was going to the National Cathedral School for Girls in Washington D.C. for her sophomore year, and she would be registering in two weeks. Not involving her in any way with decisions about her life was typical of her parents.

Happiness is like a butterfly.
The more you chase it, the more it eludes you.
But if you turn your attention to other things,
It comes and sits softly on your shoulder.
Henry David Thoreau

3. BECOMING JEANNE

1950-1954

JEANNE

What a blessing in disguise, Jeanne thought secretly after her parents dropped their bombshell on her about her future education. She had desperately wanted the chance to escape the suffocating atmosphere of her southern family with all their social rules and regulations and here was her opportunity. They in turn were delighted but amazed with their rebel daughter's acceptance of their educational plan for her. Jeanne thought she might get to know her mother a little better on their trip to school, too. However, her mother told her it was going to be an antiquing trip with Jeanne's aunts as well as a trip to her school. To Jeanne, it became the trip from hell. She hated antiques and all that they represented.

They stopped at every hamlet, town, and city along the way to Washington D.C. from Dade City, Florida. At each stop, the sisters would confer with each other endlessly about the real value of an item, where it came from and if it truly was an antique. They were completely obsessed. Everyone ignored Jeanne completely. Although used to it, it still bothered her. She decided to spend her time planning her new life. She also was anxious to know if she would be able to do the coursework, make friends and be accepted. It was very worrisome.

She had always been a fighter, something she felt she had to do to survive. Living in a family where love and affection seemed unimportant and was replaced with the worship of ancestral lineage, antiques and money, Jeanne hoped at school, she would be surrounded by people with more lofty ideals.

The minute she stepped onto campus; she felt the positive spirit of the place. Everyone was walking around with a smile on their face. The loving contagion of the school was infectious. Before she knew it, she had been drawn into the atmosphere. Something she had been looking for all her life. Her prayers to Spirit had been answered. She was home.

However nice the atmosphere of the school was, Jeanne had spent her school years battling bullies and was afraid that it would be just her luck to get a bully as a roommate. Consequentially, she asked to room alone, and her wish was granted.

The rules of the school were reasonable. In fact, she had much more freedom to grow up than her parents had ever given her. Her school year was continually enriched with the theater arts: ballet, opera, plays, and concerts, all of which were a part of the school's curriculum. She wondered why her parents, who were financially very able, had never taken her to any plays or concerts.

Sports had always been important to her and at The Cathedral, she gloried in them. She became the head cheerleader for many of the sporting events held at the school, even though the pain in her feet was excruciating, as she performed.

Her personal sporting favorites were synchronized swimming and playing on the tennis team. In swimming, her feet felt fine. In tennis, she ignored the pain.

But English classes were her bug-a-boo. Many a day, her eyes filled with tears, as she tried to write a composition that would be acceptable to her teacher and knowing she couldn't.

All her teachers were excellent. They explained the material well, were fair with their grading, and genuinely wanted her to do well. They gave willingly of their time to help her after class throughout the year.

At the end of each marking period, the school would send her parents a report on her progress, urging them to allow Jeanne to attend to a special class for extra help in English. The reply always came back with a firm no. Her mother also called the school to register her complaint that the school was implying Jeanne wasn't very intelligent by suggesting a special class for her. Her mother blamed her poor grades in English on her rebelliousness. When the headmistress tried to explain that many young people had problem areas that were difficult for them, but it had no bearing on their intelligence, Jeanne's parents turned a blind eye. Jeanne continued to struggle the rest of her sophomore and junior year.

Coming from public schools with boys and girls, Jeanne had always enjoyed young boyfriends, but at an all-girls' school, she didn't have the choices she had grown up with, in public school. She dated Vernon Spaulding her sophomore year, an egotistical, obnoxious fellow who most of her friends disliked intensely. In her junior year, she and a group of her girlfriends went to tea dances at Annapolis. It was there that she met Joe Steadman who never forgot her.

Like all teenagers, enjoying their newfound freedom, Jeanne and Mimi, her new roommate, kicked up their heels a little and were caught smoking. Their housemother didn't like them both, called them troublemakers, and cautioned them to behave in a suitable manner for young ladies. They didn't mean to purposely make her angry, they were just full of fun, laughed a lot, were noisy and ran down the halls calling to their friends as they went.

All their hi-jinks fun brought them closer together. Spending long hours discussing spirituality and what it meant to them helped them bond and become life-long friends. They were regular visitors at the priests' offices at The Cathedral. Like the young priest who confirmed Jeanne, the priests introduced them to looking at their religion in a more metaphysical way. Their explanations were far more satisfying than the explanations by the teachers in the required religious courses.

Jeanne became a sponge soaking up the beautiful hymns that were a part of the morning services in The Cathedral. She wouldn't miss them if she could help it. It was a part of her life that she had always wanted and had never been given the opportunity to have, before.

As much as she loved the music, the most important part of the service to Jeanne was communion. It was where she felt she could connect with her soul. The act of drinking the wine and eating the wafer opened her soul so she could receive and communicate directly to Spirit.

She also loved the silence the school offered in their chapels. One of her favorite things to do was go to her favorite chapel, close her eyes, and listen to her breathing in the silence. It was at those times that she also felt connected with Spirit. The feeling of love that permeated the chapel and the school made it an absolute pleasure for her to be there.

Academically, Jeanne limped through her sophomore and junior year, but at the end of her junior year, Jeanne refused to take the SATs for college entrance. She was afraid she'd fail English.

Before school closed for the summer of her junior year, Jeanne was called into,

Headmistress Leighton's office. Jeanne knew she was going to be asked about her refusal, but instead the headmistress said, "Jeanne, I regret telling you this very much because you have been a pleasure to have here, we all love you and have watched you mature into a fine young lady, but you can't come back next year."

"But why?" Jeanne asked, choking back her tears.

"Because you have had a difficult time in English and have such low scores that it would be unfair to you for you to continue."

"I will bring them up, if you let me come back! I will do everything to pass. Please give me another chance Jeanne cried out, wiping her eyes with her hands.

"Well, I'll talk to your parents when they come to pick you up for the summer and they will have to agree to send you to summer school, this summer. If you do that, we'll give you another chance."

Her mother was alone when she came to pick up Jeanne. Her father was too busy.

The head mistress had called Nell and said she needed to speak to Nell when she came.

"Have you been rebellious?"

"No mother, I love this place," Jeanne replied as they walked to the office.

"Mrs. Greenfield, I wanted to meet with you to emphasize, personally how much we love Jeanne and want the best for her at Cathedral. She has been a fine student and athlete, never needing any discipline. However, she has one weak area which we feel will keep her from graduating next year from our school. She failed English this year. As we have strongly urged you all along to allow us to give her extra help in in English and writing skills, and you have consistently refused, I must tell you that Jeanne will not be permitted to return next fall. "I feel, head mistress Leighton, Jeanne is capable, she is just lazy"........

"Mrs. Greenfield, I must interrupt. Jeanne isn't lazy. She had done well in her other subjects, been our head cheer leader, a fine choir member and a credit to our school. She just needs additional help in English," Miss Leighton said, loudly looking firmly at Nell with her eyes, blazing.

Knowing that she had met her match, Nell said, much more sweetly, "What can we do so Jeanne can come back?"

"You must send her to summer school and the school we recommend is in Miami. In fact, it is the only one that we do recommend."

Subdued, Nell gave the headmistress her promise that she would personally see that Jeanne attended summer school that summer.

On the way home, Nell said, curtly, "Jeanne, we expect you to buckle down and learn whatever it is you need to know to be able to go back to The Cathedral, next fall. You realize that I will have to drive you there every day all summer long," her tone of voice, angry and resigned.

Jeanne didn't say a word. She knew better, but she thought, if you had allowed me to have special help these past two years, you wouldn't have to drive me to Miami all summer. It's called cause and effect, a universal law, according to the priests. You caused your own problem by not allowing them to help me and the effect is you will drive me all summer.

After summer school, armed with a new body of English knowledge, Jeanne returned to her beloved school as a senior, ready to pass English. Her life changed dramatically in a way she could never have imagined. She found a spiritual phone line to Spirit and her angels. It all started that first day in English class. She was assigned an essay to write and suddenly decided to go to her favorite chapel instead of the noisy study hall. She needed spiritual help. She felt more confident than she ever had because of summer school, but years of failure had taken their toll.

The moment she entered the chapel, she was filled with a knowing that she wasn't alone and all she needed to do was to ask for help and she would get it. She opened her notebook, took out her pencil and began to write. It came so easily. It was a miracle and felt so wonderful, her eyes filled with tears. She wrote and wrote. When she looked at her watch and realized an hour had gone by, she couldn't believe it. She tucked her essay into her notebook and floated out of the chapel.

Her teacher had a huge smile on her face when she handed Jeanne her graded essay. She saw a great big fat 'A' at the top of the page and a note of congratulations. Jeanne sat down, thrilled, and stunned with tears rolling down her cheeks. After all the years of failure, she had finally written a fine article.

From then on, Jeanne would immediately go to the chapel with every writing assignment. The words came easily to form the sentences that made the paragraphs appear on her page. When she would reread her paper, it was always perfect. With each 'A' or 'B,' her confidence grew. She always thanked Spirit and her angels before she left, knowing that they had been there every moment for her. Although, she only had an inkling of her faith, it was the beginning of Jeanne' s opening to channeling knowledge and the ability to heal from Spirit which she would understand years, later. All she knew during her senior year was her newfound ability from the Universe helped her write her stories and essays.

During the year, she met a boy named Zygmunt Lee Talbot The Third from Lehigh University in Pennsylvania. He was an unusual young man who had some spiritual advice for her. Perhaps, Spirit had sent him to her, she didn't know, but she liked the fact he talked about Faith. He quoted a verse from the Bible which said, If your faith were only the size of a mustard seed, it would be large enough to uproot a mulberry tree. He gave her a pretty little, clear nugget on a chain with a mustard seed inside. His present to her was one of the most profound gifts she had ever received, delivered to her at the exact moment she needed it.

He offered to help her write her final theme on Paul and the Corinthians. During the writing, she was so moved by his written words that she spent time in the library learning all she could about Spirituality.

That year after she had met Zygmunt, a song entitled Faith Can Move Mountains, came out which said, "Darling, I can move mountains if you have faith in me," and she immediately thought of Zygmunt. The inspiration Jeanne felt when she listened to it produced some deep feelings about spirits or angels always around her. She decided that if she never had another friend on the earth, she had a host of spiritual beings on the other side that were there to help her.

Throughout Jeanne's teen-age years, at the Cathedral, she unknowingly followed southern culture's prescription for wealthy young women. She flirted outrageously with numerous young men whom she dated, although her liaisons were innocent. The men expected nothing more than a kiss from her, even though they wished for more.

In the cadre of Jeanne's young boyfriends, Jimmy Huffey, a senior from Suwanee

University was one whom she saw periodically during her senior year. In the spring, he asked her to meet him in Atlanta for a special dance. She loved the idea. It was exciting to be going to Atlanta, stay with her aunt and see Jimmy. After she got her aunt's invitation to come, Jeanne bought an airline ticket.

When her parents found out, they forbad her to go, but Jeanne ignored their orders and said she was going. They met her in Atlanta and spoiled the whole weekend. Her father said he didn't trust her. He hadn't since her fifth grade.

Undaunted by her parents to keep them apart, romantic Jimmy came to her graduation expressing his love for her.

A letter from her past arrived just before graduation on May 25, 1954. Gerald Claire wrote to say that he wanted to visit her during his senior trip to Washington D.C. Although they had a wonderful time together, it wasn't the same as it had been when they were younger. Each needed to go their separate ways and follow their own paths.

After graduation, Jeanne lived with her parents who had recently moved to Bradenton, Florida. Neal was the president of a bank there, thanks to Nell. He had borrowed the money from her to buy the controlling interest in the bank and become president. Always a shrewd businesswoman she had required that he sign a note to that effect.

Nell Leigh returned to Bradenton that summer met and

married a Scotsman named Bill McCampbell in early summer. The wedding was a huge affair with a dozen or more bridesmaids and groomsmen. It was there that Jeanne met Dick Peters. His mother had been invited to the wedding and he had come by to take her home. Seeing such a beauty, he asked Jeanne out on a date, soon afterwards, and they began a friendship that lasted for years.

Dick worked in a bank, loved being with Jeanne, but her father felt Dick would never amount to anything, but years later, Dick proved him wrong. He became a millionaire. Neal went to great lengths to make it difficult for Dick to see Jeanne. He insisted that Jeanne keep strict hours and once ordered her home from a dance at 11:30 even though Jeanne felt that as a soon-to- be college freshman, she was old enough to stay out at least until the dance was over.

When she went to Florida State in the fall, Dick went to the University of Florida. They saw each other from time to time when Jeanne could fit him into social schedule. Free of parental supervision, Jeanne became a juggler. She kept the men in her life rotating around her like balls in the air. Sometimes she cancelled a date with one to see someone else she preferred. Jimmy was one of her casualties. She called and cancelled his visit, so she could date see Dick at the University of Florida.

When Jeanne learned that he was also dating a girl who was dying, she had long talks with him about spending more time with his dying friend. Dick respected Jeanne's suggestion and was with his girlfriend until she died. Dick turned out to be a friend for Jeanne who was always there whenever he could help her.

After college, he married a girl he met at college after Jeanne had confessed that she could never marry him. She knew she would always remember him for his thoughtful and generous ways.

Uncertainty is the only certainty there is, and knowing how to live with insecurity is the only security.   John Allen Paulos

4. LIFE WITH MICHAEL

1954-1970

JEANNE

Graduating from high school was a huge accomplishment for Jeanne. She had conquered her fear of failing academically, her faith had deepened immensely, and she was more confident than she had ever been.

She wanted to go to Hollins College in Roanoke Virginia but didn't trust her ability to pass the English section of the SAT tests required. Added to that, her father wanted her to go to a school where she could learn something to help her get a job in business when she graduated.

He had said that her sister, Nell Leigh had gone to Sweet Briar, majored in sociology, was valedictorian of her class, and hadn't used her degree. But he was wrong. Nell Leigh was an exemplary straight 'A' student who landed a good job in New York City with Peck and Peck, a prestigious clothing firm because of her outstanding college record.

Typical of her parents' unwillingness to be realistic about Jeanne's capabilities, they enrolled her in the huge Florida State University as a secretarial/ business major. Going from The Cathedral's program of tender treatment for their students, Jeanne was lost in a student body of thousands. The day she tried to register, she was so confused and overwhelmed, she sat down and cried.

After the first marking period, in the fall, the Dean called her into his office. "Miss Greenfield, it's been brought to my attention that you are failing English and your teacher can't understand why after the English grades on your transcript from The Cathedral indicate that you were an 'A' student your senior year. Were you?" he asked.

Jeanne knew immediately what he was inferring: "I got an 'A' in English because I did not write those papers." Jeanne thought: "I felt inspired there, Spirit helped me write. I don't feel good here."

"What seems to be the problem?"

"In English lecture hall, I'm in a class of hundreds. Sometimes, I can't hear the professor or see everything he is writing on the blackboard. At times in the small classes, the professor never shows up. The Teacher's Assistant that teaches us, he's not very good!" Jeanne said, defensively, her arms crossed.

"Uh, well," the Dean paused, "I'm sure OUR professors are doing a good job, Miss Greenfield. What was the difference at The Cathedral?"

"The teachers cared about me and let me write my essays in the chapel on campus. It was quiet and I was able to write there, easily. I spent the summer before in summer school learning English skills and I did write those essays myself!"

The Dean looked at her and said, "Very well, Miss Greenfield, perhaps, we can excuse this first grade, but I suggest you find a quiet place here to do your writing and do a good job."

Jeanne walked out of the Dean's office, pleased that she had staunchly stood her ground and he had finally believed her.

That fall, besides dealing with the culture shock of a big, huge university, Jeanne had to cope with all the sororities 'rushing' her. Having lived all over Florida, she knew most of the members of the different sorority houses. She also knew that her wide circle of female relatives had written to their sororities encouraging them to ask her to join. The result was she received many sororities written invitations, called 'bids,' to join their sorority.

But it was a different story for her roommate, Shirley. When the bids were delivered, she didn't receive one. Even Jeanne's friend, the president of Chi Omega who had promised Shirley a bid didn't follow through. It made Jeanne furious. She knew how it felt to be left out and labeled all the sorority women, 'judging bitches.' She thought, some things never change, they were like the women she had known her whole life and she disliked them. But she found it hard to say no to them.

She solved that problem by flunking English. No sorority was allowed to initiate student who had failed a course. It was also a relief for Jeanne to be left alone. When Jeanne met two more girls at the university whom she had known and liked since she was young who hadn't received bids, she wasn't surprised. They didn't fit the social mold.

All through the fall, Jeanne attracted men to her like bees to honey. She was beautiful, flirted a lot, full of fun and ready for anything. As before, she continued the pattern that all young, wealthy southern girls followed of teasing her boyfriends, making them desire her, but keeping her innocence. She was good at it and without realizing what she was doing, she was mimicking her mother's behavior pattern when she was young.

Another side of Jeanne rebelled against the social pressure of the southern culture by buying and wearing a cap that had bells on it and wore it everywhere. She would shake her head and make the bells ring when she met women she didn't like. The startled expression on their faces delighted her.

Michael was one of her boyfriends. He was a junior at Clemson. Jeanne had known him since the fifth grade and had grown up with him. His sister, Mary Alice, had been her best friend. Michael began dating her in earnest the summer before she went to college. Her friends said he resembled Paul

Newman, was charming, fun to be with, but her intuition cautioned her about him. At first, Jeanne took him lightly. Part of her thought of him as a brother, having known him since they were kids. Through Michael's persistence, they dated all through her freshman year. Gradually, they had more and more steamy, passionate interludes in his car. One evening in June, Jeanne came dangerously close to having intercourse with him, but stopped short of the actual act. Michael was so excited, his semen leaked all over her underwear.

A month later when she didn't have a period and was feeling nauseated, she knew she was pregnant. Her mind screamed; how could this happen? I didn't have relations with Michael. What am I going to do? My parents have given me a trip to Europe with my cousin and it's all set. How can I tell them I'm pregnant? That's easy, I won 't. But she was and it made the month-long trip a trying experience.

Before she left, her parents reminded her to look for the name, Talbot. "We are directly related to the Earl of Talbot through my father's side of the family," her father said, proudly.

"And don't forget the Edwards name," Nell interjected. "My mother's mother was his direct descendent." It was obvious how important her parents felt about their lineage.

Jeanne and her cousin were to cross the Atlantic on the ship Queen Elizabeth, but at the last moment, the ship workers struck, and they had to fly instead, landing in Paris instead of London. Before they had gone, Nell had sent Jeanne to an astrologer who warned Jeanne about traveling across large bodies of water by boat. The strike had taken care of that problem.

They were met by a charming French tour guide who took an immediate interest in Jeanne. All the time they were in France, he paid special attention to her and took her and her cousin on interesting tours. It pleased and amused Jeanne. She charmed him in the way only a southern belle could.

While in England, during one of their stops on the travel

bus, Jeanne recognized the name of Talbot on a bank and down the street was the Edwards Company. She laughed when she realized both of her parents' ancestor's names were a stone's throw from each other.

One day, halfway through the trip, feeling particularly sick and worried, she decided she needed to tell Michael about the pregnancy. She found a telegraph office and sent a telegram that read: Congratulations, you are going to be a father, Jeanne.

Michael told her when she returned that when the construction foreman delivered the telegram to him in person, he was working on the top of a building. His boss had said, as he handed it to him, "I hope it isn't bad news." When Michael read it, he nearly fell off the building.

Worried, all through the trip, Jeanne kept thinking of ways to tell her father about her pregnancy. Back from the trip, she had worked up enough courage to talk to him, she felt she needed to take it slow and start by asking to get engaged, first.

Her father looked at her as if she had asked for one of his kidneys and said, "I can't believe that a daughter of mine wants to marry a Catholic. You know how your mother and I feel about Catholics. You would be marrying beneath your class. Irish Catholics are not one of us. Furthermore, I forbid you to ever see Michael again, much less marry him."

"You'll be sorry you said that" Jeanne replied, angrily.

"Father, just because his family isn't in the southern social register, they are good people. Maybe his grandfather wasn't a general in the War Between the States, but he is an intelligent man. He's going to graduate from Clemson next year."

"There will be no more discussion about this, Jeanne," her father replied. When Jeanne left the room, Nell said, "I can't believe our daughter is considering marrying Michael. His family ancestors were probably convicts from Ireland who came here as indentured servants. While we, who can trace our lineage back to the Earl of Talbot, and the Earl who is probably turning over in his grave in England thinking about our daughter marrying an Irishman."

In desperation, a few days later, she went to Michael to tell him that her father and mother turned her down flat on their engagement.

Not really listening to her, Michael said, shaking his head, "I don't understand it. How did you get pregnant?"

"I don't know, but I am, and this baby wants to be born. Maybe your sperm were good swimmers or maybe it's an Immaculate Conception," Jeanne-replied, only half-way kidding.

"So, what do you want to do?" Michael asked, looking, and sounding unhappy.

"I think we have to get married next month before you go back to school."

He stood outside her house, kicking the dirt with his shoe, silently. He finally looked at her and said, "I never planned on this. It's hard to think of being married, right now."

"How do you think I feel? I never planned this either! Do you think I like being pregnant and not married? There is no other way, Michael, and you know it!"

"Okay, okay, don't yell at me. We'll just tell them we're getting married, and I'll tell my mom," he said, dejectedly.

"I'll tell my parents, alone. It will be better, I think."

After getting Michael's reluctant okay, she announced to her parents that she and Michael were getting married in August because she was pregnant.

"Jeanne, I know a very good doctor who does,........ uh, abortions," her father said, quietly.

"No, father, I won't do that. I want this baby. There is a reason she is coming."

Michael and Jeanne decided to elope to Georgia and get

married in August. They had to send for Nell and Syd to come and sign for them because they were both underage.

Jeanne knew they were getting married for all the wrong reasons, but like a naive young woman, she told herself, It will work out, I will make it happen. And besides, I have no other choice.

They were married in Georgia in August 1954 by a justice of the peace in a hurried ceremony, accompanied by Nell and Michael's mother Syd. No one was very happy, especially Michael.

Right from the beginning, their marriage was built on shaky ground. Although both were very intelligent, Michael was struggling with an undiagnosed inherited alcohol addiction from a chemical called THIQ and years later when Jeanne tried to tell his father, Francis, that his son was an alcoholic, he wouldn't believe it and was never friendly towards Jeanne after that.

Jeanne's problem was undiagnosed Dyslexia, an inherited trait making it difficult for her to read and write easily. They were young. She was eighteen, nauseated with her pregnancy and self-conscious. He was twenty, a reluctant bridegroom, father of her baby and silently ignoring his marriage.

Jeanne had gone to a reader a few months before to learn anything she could about her future husband. She had told her that she and her present mother had been sisters in a past life and Michael was to marry her mother, but fell in love with her instead, married her and they had a baby boy named Neal. Michael went to the Civil War, deserted, and left Jeanne and their baby, forever.

That old principle of cause and effect kept popping up, again and again in Jeanne's life. Michael caused their present situation by deserting her in a past life and the effect was being forced to marry her in this life because of her pregnancy. But she learned that he abandoned her before, and he was well on his way to doing the same thing to her again in this life.

Jeanne's mantra which she would repeat hundreds of times during their marriage was: "I'm going to make my marriage work." She used it two days after the ceremony. Michael had disappeared. Jeanne knew he had fled to see his current girlfriend. Monogamy for Michael was an impossibility.

There was no honeymoon. After the wedding, they stayed with Michael's mother in Sarasota until it was time for him to return to school. This time he was bringing his pregnant wife with him. They moved into married housing, and Michael became a student again and was always gone. Although he had perfectly legitimate excuses, Jeanne wondered if he was spending time with a girl, somewhere. He was quick with his alibi, saying he spent his days in the classroom, library, and the rest of the time, practicing with the football team. Jeanne was nauseated, lonely and away from her family and friends and blamed Michael.

That fall, Clemson went co-ed and Jeanne was there to witness it. Previously, it had been a military school that had become an all-male institution. Bowing to financial pressure, Clemson opened its doors to women.

All kinds of stories circulated around the new women who were the first women to attend the classes as co-eds. One story Jeanne heard involved a young lady who had enrolled in a psychology course and was the first and only woman in the class. As the professor called roll, when he called her name, he stopped, looked up and said, "Young lady will you please cross your legs." She did and he said, "Good, now that the gates of hell have been closed, we can proceed with the roll call," in a truly chauvinistic style.

Jeanne and Michael chaperoned dances in the Catholic Church and made friends with other young people there. It always seemed odd to Jeanne that Michael would involve himself with his church and ignore its rules about chasing with women, but he did. He had two personalities.

One day, two nuns knocked on her door and said that they were conducting a survey.

"For the survey, is your husband Catholic?" Jeanne nodded to the affirmative.

"Are you Catholic?"

"No," Jeanne replied.

"Do you have

any children?"

"Yes, one girl."

"Has she been baptized?"

"Yes," Jeanne said, firmly.

"Well, don't you think you should join the Catholic Church?"

Jeanne was about at the end of her patience, and she answered, "If you mention one more word about me becoming a Catholic, you will cause a divorce in our family, and I know you don't like Catholics being divorced. It's best you leave," she stated, angrily.

One night, Michael decided it was their turn to have a party and proceeded to make some alcoholic punch using pure alcohol from the zoology lab. It was so powerful that Michael's professor got so drunk he fell down a flight of steps and couldn't come to class for two weeks. No one said a thing about it when he did return.

That year was hard for them for many reasons. They were both very young and inexperienced trying to live together. She hated Michael a lot of the time because he acted completely oblivious about her feelings and was gone more than he was home. He had a lot of friends he had made at Clemson and went out with his football buddies all the time. She found out they were going to dances and parties, alone!

She hated Clemson. It was impersonal and chauvinistic. Plus, the pregnancy made her feel nauseated all nine months and she couldn't eat much. She ended up skin and bones before the baby came, having lost thirty-six pounds. The final straw was they were always broke. Thank God for her parents who sent money to her all the time for groceries.

How to cook was something Jeanne had never learned. She had never been allowed to learn that skill from her black nanny because her mother said it was beneath her. It was one more foolish southern rule that her mother insisted upon, adding to Jeanne's feelings of inferiority. Consequently, she had a terrible time trying to make a meal. She used too much salt or not enough, she overcooked or undercooked food, plus she was always nauseated with her pregnancy. She mastered making pork chops and gravy but could hardly look at them without running to the bathroom and throwing up.

Jeanne turned to studying astrology charts in the hopes that they would provide information as to why Michael behaved the way he did. He and her father had the same sign. They were both Libras, but Michael either had no intuition or didn't use it. Her father did use his and could tell when a customer walked into his bank whether he would be a good risk or not for a loan.

Jeanne, like her father, had Scorpio rising in their horoscopes which gave her an intuitive ability, early-on to survive in school, escaping the bullies.

The months moved slowly by, and Jeanne got bigger and bigger with her pregnancy. She craved and lived on bananas and popsicles. When the first labor pains started, she was relieved to know it would soon be over, and her baby would be with her. On February 25, 1955, Jeanne delivered a beautiful baby girl at the hospital in Anderson, South Carolina. Jeanne loved her baby girl, but only she and her mother shared the excitement of a new baby. Michael was disappointed. He had wanted a boy. The day they were to leave, the nurse came in and said, "Mrs. Corrigan, you have to name the baby before you leave so she is on our records.

Jeanne knew what to name her baby. Mary Ann had told her mother before she was born, while up in the ethers, that her name was Mary Ann. While her mother and Michael were both arguing about the baby's name Jeanne stopped all discussion by saying, "I know what her name is," she told me. Her first part of her name is Mary after Jesus's mother, and the second part is Ann after Mary's mother."

When they all walked into their small apartment, there were no flowers or a card from Michael to welcome her and the baby home, there was only indifference.

Nell helped her daughter for a week or so and when she left, Syd, Michael's mother arrived and took over. It was love at first sight for both Jeanne and Mary Ann. They bonded quickly and Mary Ann was a happy baby. Nell hired a nanny before she left to start to take care of Mary Ann when Syd left.

At first, it was fine, but soon Jeanne was disgusted with the nanny's laziness. She let Mary Ann sleep all day so she didn't have to take care of her, and Jeanne would end up taking care of her wakeful baby all night long. After a week or two of that, Jeanne fired the nanny and changed Mary Ann's days and nights around so she could get some sleep at night.

When Michael finally graduated, Mary Ann was almost two and Jeanne was pregnant with their second child. Michael landed a good beginning job with Owens Company of Illinois in their glass division. The only problem was it was in Waco, Texas.

Never confiding in her and hardly really talking
to her, when Michael announced,

"We're moving to Waco, I've got a job there," Jeanne's first reactions were surprise and delight. They finally would have some money to live on, she thought. She was hopeful their life would be better. She didn't like leaving Florida, but she was ready to give Waco, Texas a try. She knew she would have to tread lightly if she registered any concerns about moving to Texas.

"It's so far away from my family and friends," she said, afraid to rock the boat. When Michael's decisions were ever questioned Jeanne could sense a hidden anger in him. "Besides," she said, "I'm sick with this pregnancy."

"And whose damn fault was that? Why weren't you more careful? Didn't you use that diaphragm of yours?" He asked, grimly, His face getting redder by the minute.

"Yes, of course I did, but this baby wants to be born and no diaphragm is going to stop him from coming."

"That's nonsense. You just need a new one. The old one leaks or doesn't fit. Go to a doctor when we get there. Two kids are enough."

"You're awful, Michael," Jeanne said, quietly,
half-afraid of Michael to say more.

"So, it's settled, then. Pack-up, and get that sister of yours to help you," he ordered, curtly.

Nauseated again with her pregnancy, the train trip to Waco was a nightmare. They would have flown, but Nell Leigh was with them at Nell's insistence and afraid to fly so they all had to ride the trains. Halfway there, they had to change trains and the second one was five hours late. Jeanne was so sick, they had to go to a hotel and rent a room for her to lie down to wait for the train. When they finally boarded, the train was reminiscent of one from the 1800's. It had rough, wooden coach seats and was 108 degrees inside with no way to cool off. There was no meal service. Halfway to Waco, the train stopped, and they got off the train for a meal. The town they ate in had wooden sidewalks. It reminded Jeanne of the cowboy movies she used to watch when she was a kid, on Saturdays.

One good thing about the trip was what a happy little girl Mary Ann was, smiling at all the men on the train. Jeanne hugged her and said, "You little flirt, you have all the men talking and smiling back at you." By the time they arrived in Waco, every man on the train had talked to her at one time or another.

Nell Leigh turned out to be a big help and comfort. She rescued Jeanne from feeling lost and overwhelmed. When Jeanne was older, she looked back on that time with Nell, the fun they had, and she knew Nell could have been one of her best friends if she hadn't been her half-sister.

When they were finally unpacked and settled, Jeanne said, "Let's go out and see Waco." They took Mary Ann and spent days investigating the city. One of the highlights they found was tours of Owen's glass factory. Fascinated with the glass making process, they would stand for hours watching the artisans mold hot blob of glass into a beautiful piece. When they were satisfied with their creations, they would send them to the store or to the furnace for the next stop. It was a magical process from beginning to end.

One day, a priest rang Jeanne's doorbell and asked to speak to her about her faith?"

"If you mention one word about me becoming a Catholic and you will cause a divorce in the family, and I know you don't like Catholics being divorced. It's best you leave."

Jeanne had to fend off that type of aggressive behavior from Catholics in every town, they lived in.

Michael worked long hours or at least that was what he told Jeanne, but Jeanne felt he was sleeping with women there, too. Jeanne had the uncanny ability to be able to pick them out in a crowd. Waco had a continuous carnival on the outskirts of town where she and Michael took Mary Ann for walks in the stroller. As they strolled along, Jeanne could spot the women

Michael had slept with without any difficulty. It was a special gift that she had.

Michael was crazy at times, especially when he had been drinking a lot. He belonged to a men's group from work and on Friday nights they would get together and go out drinking. One Friday night, he came home with a goat. He was so drunk he brought the goat into the house. It was frightened, defecated and urinated all over the living room. It took them many hours to clean the house after that episode.

After another drinking spree, Michael tore the transmission out of his car and they didn't have the money to fix it, so Jeanne's father, Neal came to the rescue and bought them another car.

One night when Jeanne returned from her trip to Florida with her children to see her family, she asked where the television had gone. Michael looked at her and said, nastily, "I loaned it to a friend for the time being. You will have to live without it."

Jeanne felt like she was on an insane merry-go-round with Michael, young and unsure of herself, she tried to cope with his escapades as well as a twenty-year-old could do. One thing she knew, she needed to find a good doctor for her and her unborn baby.

Feeling the urgency, Jeanne asked Nell Leigh to look in the phone book for a doctor. When Jeanne saw Dr. Joe Corbett, she knew he was the right doctor for her and called his office for an appointment. Nell Leigh went with her to meet him in place of Michael who gave his usual excuse saying he was too busy, working.

Waiting for the nurse to call her when they arrived, Jeanne had a burning question on her mind that needed an answer. When his nurse finally called her name, she left Nell Leigh flipping through a magazine and followed the nurse. Her first impression of Joe Corbett was good. She hoped he was as good a doctor as he was good looking. Once they began talking, Jeanne knew he was the doctor for her. He had an easy, relaxed manner with her, which made it easy to talk to him and she said what was on her mind.

"Doctor, I'm married to a Catholic and I've read that their church says if there has to be a choice to be made between the mother and the baby living, the doctor must save the baby. Are you a Catholic and do you agree with that?"

Joe sat back in his chair and said, "No, Jeanne, I was born a Baptist, raised a Catholic, and finally joined the 'Wiskopalian' Church. No church has that right to decide life or death. My main aim is to make sure you and the baby both survive."

Jeanne liked him for his answer. He had a way about him that made her feel comfortable. She could trust him. He planned for her to have her baby in the Baptist hospital explaining that that he worked out of that hospital, was familiar with the nurses and the general procedures there. She learned something else about him that she liked. He was an old-fashioned doctor who made house calls.

She delivered Neal on December 14, 1957. He was a perfect baby, but she began hemorrhaging. Joe's quick thinking saved her life. He stayed with her until he was sure she was stabilized. With that pregnancy, Jeanne's breasts became terribly sore, and her nipples began bleeding. The nurses were understanding, knew exactly what to do to help them heal and pampered Jeanne. Throughout the whole experience, Joe oversaw her recovery.

After her six weeks check-up, Joe refitted her with a new diaphragm. But two years later, Jeanne got pregnant once again. Her pregnancy again was a big surprise. She had been very careful to use protection, but another baby was on the way. Jeanne decided that Spirit wanted her to have three children. They had chosen her and Michael for their parents and nothing would prevent them from coming.

When she told Michael, he insisted she go to a Catholic hospital for the delivery. Why he was so adamant? It confused her. He, who never cared what she did if she didn't bother him, was making that decision. She wondered if his main reason for being so dictatorial was to make her miserable knowing that she loved the Baptist hospital.

Jeanne panicked and called her doctor. "Joe, Michael is insisting I go to the Catholic hospital for my delivery, and I'm scared."

Joe replied, "Don't worry, I'll deliver your baby there and make sure nothing happens to you," and he did. David was born easily; a perfect baby and Jeanne was fine.

Joe and his wife became friends with Michael and Jeanne and went to dances and parties with them. Because Joe's wife was a Native American, the white in-crowd looked down on Joe for marrying an Indian and her for being one. They were continually ostracized and ignored. Of course, Jeanne knew all about being left out and ignored and it made her more determined than ever to be their friend.

Jeanne and Mary Alice had kept in close contact over the years and Jeanne invited her to visit. She came several times and each time, Jeanne, with devilment in her heart and asked Mary Alice to go hunting with her.

"What are we looking for?" Mary Alice asked. "Michael's current girlfriend, of course" replied Jeanne.

Mary Alice laughed and asked, "I'd love to, but doesn't it upset you to see him with another woman?"Sure, but it's fun to see Michael squirm a little."

Jeanne knew all the bars Michael inhabited and together they always found him. Sometimes, right away and sometimes it took an hour or so before they got lucky.

On one of their hunting expeditions, they couldn't find him. Finally, after several tries, they went to a new bar and there he was sitting at a bar laughing with his arm around a woman. She whispered to Mary Alice, "There he is, let's go surprise him and his lady love."

Jeanne slipped up beside him and asked, in a loud voice for everyone at the bar to hear, hello my darling husband, who is this nice lady?

As smooth as silk, Michael introduced her as if it was perfectly okay to be with the girlfriend. Jeanne and Mary Alice talked with them until the woman got embarrassed and left. Either way, Jeanne enjoyed herself. The following morning Michael never mentioned the night before. It was as if it had never happened. It was a pattern he continued all through their married life.

Lonely for a real conversation with her husband, Jeanne bought his favorite drink, scotch, and bourbon for herself, put the bottles on the table in a bar room and said, "We're not leaving here until you talk to me about what's going on."

He sat there drinking, quietly, ignoring her until he finished his drink and Jeanne sadly accepted the fact that she was in a loveless marriage.

Periodically, Michael and his friends went down to Mexico, supposedly to gamble, but they wanted to find some hot prostitutes. Their plans were changed quickly when they were rolled by their prostitutes, when they were dead drunk and lost every penny, they had with them. They ended up calling a neighbor who had to send them enough money to get home.

Even though Jeanne tried to shield the children from Michael's continual, childish, and sometimes crazy behavior, they knew and felt everything that was happening with their father. With all the strife and confusion, Jeanne tried to keep their lives as normal as possible, but it was impossible because of Michael. The seeds of addiction and depression were planted in them from an early age.

Michael's quasi-favorite child was Mary Anne, but he really didn't possess any natural feelings of a father, so she didn't get much special attention. His ability to discipline or raise children was sketchy. One moment he'd be too strict and other times indifferent depending on his mood. He really didn't like any children, including his own.

One night when Jeanne was out, he threw Mary Ann out of the house in a fit of anger because she had disobeyed him and gone to a carnival. Mary Anne was just a youngster and was terrified. When Jeanne returned, Mary Ann was gone, and Jeanne had to go find her. Michael had over-reacted, and his punishment was completely uncalled for. All their children ever wanted was their father's love but were never able to reach him. Michael's continued lack of caring for his children was a big factor in the many problems they had throughout their lives.

She also knew that she wasn't the perfect mother, but she loved her children and showed it continually. Her love was the one constant in their lives. However, living in a home with a father who was a silent drunk destroyed the peace and love that they needed to thrive. They retreated into themselves, sure that they were somehow the cause of their father's behavior. As Neal grew up, he took it upon himself to protect his mother from his father. It was a terrible position, but he insisted on being her protector.

One day, the phone rang. It was her mother, sounding upset. Nell demanded that Jeanne come home, immediately because her father was in the hospital and very sick. Promising to come as soon as she could, Jeanne called the airlines for a ticket, packed up Mary Ann and Neal and left for the airport that day. At home, she found her mother bedridden with grief.

She settled the children with the babysitter and left for the hospital.

The night before he died, Jeanne knew he would be making his transition soon. She sat quietly with him in his room, listening to his labored breathing and reminiscing about their life together. She had some good memories of them together, some very angry ones and some that were confusing to her. She couldn't explain them to herself. In a weak, soft voice, so unlike him when he was well, he said, "Jeanne, I want you to bring your mother to see me tomorrow. I'm not going to last very long." He died soon after he saw his wife.

Jeanne went to a reader who told Jeanne that her father wanted to be cremated with as little fuss as possible. To back up what the psychic reader had said, Jeanne went to her mother and asked, "Mother, did dad want to be cremated?"

"Yes, but I'd never do that. He needs to be honored in a normal funeral. All our friends want to come to view his body and know he will be buried with all his relatives in a normal grave site."

Jeanne knew that her mother's life had been steeped in doing things the proper southern way including burial etiquette. Cremation was just beginning to be accepted, but not by good southern families. The idea of burning up a beloved family member was abhorrent to them. And Jeanne knew her mother wanted a 'social funeral' where she could reign as queen bee and have hundreds of condolences given to her by all of her friends.

Jeanne called Michael and said, "Michael, please come as soon as you can. Dad died, last night. Nell Leigh and her husband just left on an inconvenient business trip, mother is distraught, so I have to make all the arrangements."

"Your father's death changes everything for me. I need to talk to Nell when I'm up there about the loan that your father promised me. I need the money to start my business. I want to move back to Jacksonville, Florida. You'd like that wouldn't you, being near your family?"

"Don't do anything foolish, Michael. Hurry up here."

Jeanne missed her father's stabilizing presence to the family. The patriarch was gone, and everyone felt it. When Michael came, Jeanne still had hope for their marriage. The following month, she knew she was pregnant. She couldn't believe it. Their baby was bound and determined to be born, even with her precautionary efforts of using a diaphragm.

Michael's timing was poor, asking Nell to honor her husband's offer of a loan to him, at that time. Nell had turned him down, flat. Jeanne knew her mother didn't think their marriage would last and used that as an excuse.

Hurt and angry, to escape for a little while, Michael made plans to go to a Red Sox game. Jeanne asked him not to go because she felt he should be with the family. He got so mad at her he got roaring drunk and stayed mad at her and her family for two weeks.

But Michael made it plain that he was going back to Florida. When they returned to Waco three days after the funeral, he told his boss he wanted a transfer to the Jacksonville corrugated box plant of Owens of Illinois Glass Company. While that was being arranged, Michael was not to be deterred and contacted Jeanne's uncle, asking him for a loan of five thousand dollars. Michael had plans to start a corrugated box company of his own in Jacksonville.

Their third child, David, was born December 27, 1959. When she called Michael's parents, full of excitement, about their latest grandchild, they insisted she would promise to make a family visit in the early spring to see the baby and their other two grandchildren.

Michael and Jeanne made the mistake of renting a home too small for their family in Jacksonville. The company moved their belongings to the tiny house and Jeanne followed. Just recovering from having her baby, David, and with two other active children Jeanne hated their house. It was bursting at the seams with all their furniture. Jeanne was alone and depressed dealing with her new cramped surroundings and her demanding family.

Miserable, she wrote an emotional letter to Michael and asked for a divorce. In his reply, he asked her not to leave him and promised to get her a bigger home for their family when he came. Because of Michael's past dalliances and his seeming lack of any real feelings for her she couldn't understand why he still wanted to stay married to her. An ugly thought kept gnawing at her. Did Michael stay with her because he was still counting on money from her mother? She was certainly sure it wasn't because he loved her, or was it?

When Michael followed two months later, he afforded them a much larger home which Jeanne loved. Michael went to work in the corrugated box plant and made plans to work for himself.

As she had promised, in April, she packed the car and put Mary Ann, Neal and the baby in there and drove to Dade City from Jacksonville in one day to see Michael's parents. She was glad to arrive, safe and sound with her precious crew and thanked Spirit for her safe trip.

Once there, she walked into a room full of black robes. It was a convention of Catholic priests. Her mother-in-law loved to entertain, especially the priests. As she stood there waiting to be introduced, she saw a tall, handsome, red-haired priest among the group. Who was he? She wondered. I feel like I've known him before. The instant attraction between them was so strong she could hardly breathe. When Syd introduced her to him as Father Peter, Jeanne thought, I've got to get out of here, and she left the room to collect her wits.

After she returned from her trip, she was more discontented than before. It made her really question the superficiality of their marriage. The only validity the marriage had produced was her three children. No matter what happened between her and Michael, she loved those children with her whole heart. They were healthy, beautiful children but Michael, unfortunately, seemed oblivious to them. Jeanne's mantra that she prayed daily had changed. Now it was "I will prove to you that I can make it work." Her rebellious attitude in lots of circumstances had hurt her over the years and she was beginning to realize that.

Michael was working hard starting their new box company. After a couple of years and the company was running fairly well, Michael wanted a change and a vacation. He had always dreamed of crewing on a racing star boat and decided to try his hand at it. It was a whole new experience for Michael, and he thrived on exciting, new adventures.

Becoming confident as a crew member when his boat had won some races, he invited Jeanne to come to New Orleans, to watch him race and join in his excitement. She agreed, pleased that he had invited her to be with him. She left the children with their nanny and flew to New Orleans.

The night they flew home, Jeanne was happily looking out the plane's tiny window when she saw the flames of a huge fire coming from an area close to the airport.

"Michael, is that our plant burning?" She asked, shocked with the thought.

He looked out and said, "It certainly is!

"What can we do?"

"Nothing, but collect the insurance," he remarked, nonchalantly.

His lawyer confirmed her suspicions after Michael died. Michael had hired someone to set fire to his two other companies so he could collect the insurance. Needing more money, he hired an arsonist to repeat his scheme again with a third fire. However, this time someone was hurt. No negligence could be proved on Michael's part and everyone in the family knew he had sold the remains of the plant to the Mafia for money laundering. The culprit who did it was too clever to be caught and left no incriminating evidence.

With his insurance money, Michael started a new folding box plant in Jacksonville. Jeanne went to work helping him get started. One day, after she arrived, she learned that someone had thrown a rock through the window during the night. Jeanne intuitively knew that whoever did it was mad at Michael.

Speaking as a mother, to protect her children, she bravely confronted him. "Michael, I don't know what you've done to have this kind of thing happen but fix it. I don't want our children exposed to things like this."

Michael gave her an angry look, but he understood her ultimatum and didn't argue with her. That never happened again.

Michael's mother had always naturally expected Jeanne to raise their children as Catholics, continually making Jeanne aware of her wishes. Growing up as an Episcopalian, Jeanne had naturally raised her children as she had been raised and took them to her church every Sunday.

But under pressure from Syd, she reluctantly enrolled Mary Ann in her first communion class. When Mary Ann came home one day from class, she burst into tears and said, "Mommy, Sister Angelina said you were going to hell because you aren't a Catholic."

"Well, Sister Angelina is wrong. I'm going right up to heaven with all of you. Mom isn't going to leave you all that easily."

She hugged Mary Ann and said, "Now, get ready for supper and don't think another thing about it."

The next day, Jeanne went to see the Catholic bishop, an old friend of hers and told him Mary Ann's grim story. The following week when Mary Ann came home from class, she was happy. Jeanne learned later that the bishop had been furious when he visited the mother superior and told her Jeanne's story. It was obvious the mother superior had spoken to Sister Angelina.

While Michael owned his folding box company, he also bought a restaurant in Jacksonville and named it the Green Derby. It was essentially a sports bar with two additional rooms. The whole place was redecorated beautifully, each room with its own special décor. The middle room, for families, with its tables covered with white cloths, and set with quality glassware and expensive table settings, it had the look of a lovely dining room. It was the only room without a bar. The other adjacent room was set up with a beautiful piano as the centerpiece.

Michael hired a good pianist to play every night. The main room resembled a high-class nightclub, complete with tables, indirect lighting, and a beautiful bar with mirrors everywhere.

Michael spared no expense to produce the effect he wanted. With the decorating skill of Jeanne's mother and her friends, the place was gorgeous.

Michael hired two men to run the restaurant during the day while he worked at his company and in the evenings, the three of them ran it, together. The energy that Michael had to expend on both jobs was unbelievable. He was like a human dynamo who seemed to have an unending source of money to spend on the restaurant. Jeanne had no idea how much he spent or cleared each year and he never offered to share that information with her.

When the restaurant opened, Michael wanted her there with him in the evenings and she tolerated being there. It was a seamy slice of life that was far different from her background and life up until then.

She made up her mind that she wasn't going to make

her children suffer with their father's new restaurant venture. She always, fed her children, read them stories, tucked them in for the evening, and then dressed for the evening. Leaving the nanny with instructions to call her if one of the children needed her, Jeanne went to work at the restaurant.

Besides the legitimate business of serving food and drink, Jeanne felt there was a mystery about the place. She had her suspicions and by making friends with the waitresses, she soon learned that all kinds of shady deals including prostitution and gambling were going on there all the time behind closed doors up-stairs.

The waitresses loved to gossip to her about the clientele. Their stories included navy wives who worked as prostitutes, making money for vacations with their husbands when they returned from a tour of duty, wealthy high rollers, the Mafia, and others from the underworld who ran high stakes gambling games up-stairs. It was understood that Michael took a percentage of everything.

One of the funniest things happened one night that almost shut their place down by the Jacksonville board of health. Michael was nowhere to be found that particular night. Jeanne needed him to help her persuade and escort a very drunk and obnoxious woman out to her taxi using his charm. Where was that husband of mine when I need him? She wondered. "Where have you been?" Jeanne asked when he sauntered in from outside.

"I've been talking with a horse trader."

"A horse trader, what for?"

"We're going to have a horse in here to entertain the crowd."

"You can't do that; you'll be shut down when the board of health hears about it."

"Don't tell me what I can or can't do," Michael replied, stubbornly.

The next thing Jeanne knew, a man was leading a horse into the club. All conversation stopped, and everyone became very quiet and watched with fascination as the horse's owner put his horse through his tricks. The horse drank a beer, danced, bent down on his front knees, and bowed and took the owner's hat off his head with his teeth.

The next morning, the radio talk shows were all talking about the horse act at the Green Derby.

That night, Michael surprised Jeanne with plans he had for her. In his most charming manner, he said, "Now, that we are really rolling, I need you to help bring customers to the bar so they will spend their money by sitting there looking gorgeous. I've bought you some dresses that will knock 'em dead and I want you to wear plenty of makeup, the kind that makes your face look really exciting. I don't want you to look old and washed-out." He paused for a moment and said, "Even though you have a big ass and skinny legs, the rest of your body is good," and laughed.

Jeanne didn't like the whole idea, even though she knew Michael was proud of her looks and wanted to show her off to the clientele. He gave her the excuse that she added to the club with her presence which was good for the success of their restaurant. She was flattered that he wanted to show her off, but when she put on one of the dresses, she was shocked when she looked in the mirror. Her breasts were so exposed she thought if I bend over, they'll fall out of my dress. I look like a whore. But foolishly, she said to herself, give it a chance, maybe it will be all right.

Adding to her discomfort, Jeanne was battling a painful disease called endometriosis which caused terrible cramps. Although basically healthy most of her young life, endometriosis had slowly developed before her three children were born, making her life miserable, physically during her periods. She was told by her OB/GYN doctors that it was usually impossible to get pregnant with that disease, but that had never been her problem.

In June of 1964, Jeanne had a hysterectomy to stop the disease from spreading. As she recovered from surgery at home, her life slowed down, forcing her to think about her life. When she recovered, she made a decision that she knew would infuriate Michael, but she didn't care. She wasn't going to act a part to please Michael, anymore.

One day, Nell Leigh asked, "How are you feeling since the operation?"

"Okay, but it's been slow."

"Do you want to go out tonight to the club? I have a couple of friends visiting and I'd like to show them the Green Derby."

"Sure, I need a change."

"Good, we'll pick you up at 8:00."

Jeanne perked up and chose a pretty cocktail dress that she liked with a normal neckline. She was ready and waiting outside when Nell Leigh drove up.

The minute Michael saw them come in, he came over, gave Jeanne an impatient look and said, "I want to talk to you." They moved away from Jeanne's guests, and he said, "As long as you are here, get up to the bar and entertain the customers."

Jeanne thought, I hate the way Michael talks to me, sometimes, ordering me around. She said, "No, I'll never wear another low-cut dress, nor wear a face-full of make-up and sit at the bar like a whore for you. I'm finished," she said, her eyes flashing with anger.

Michael reacted and said angrily, "I never want you to act inappropriately, I just want you to help entertain the guests. I'm here every night working my ass off and I expect you to help, too."

"Michael, I'm your wife and we have three children if you remember."

Michael turned on his heel and walked away.

Nell and her friends knew that Jeanne and Michael had been fighting, they read the body language from across the room. When Jeanne returned and sat down with them, her face was red with anger, and she quickly ordered a martini.

After her big fight, Jeanne continued to come to the Derby in a much different capacity. She enjoyed mingling with the guests, talking and making them feel welcome, but she never sat at the bar again.

Because of all the people that they met at the Green Derby, all of the friends that they both had in Jacksonville, Michael and Jeanne were invited out to many dinner parties. Sometimes, they were terribly boring parties because of the reserved personalities who hosted the evenings. On one particular night, they were invited to the home of some very proper friends. Met at the door by the host and hostess dressed to the nines, the lady of the house had on a formal, full-length gown and her husband was wearing a smoking jacket. Jeanne knew from Michael's remarks he was going to do something to enliven the evening.

As the evening wore on with everyone sitting out on their patio eating and drinking, Michael got up and left the party. After a few minutes, he returned in his briefs wearing the hostess's night gown. He walked in as if he always wore female nightgowns, talked to everyone until he was drowned out by the gales of laughter from everyone. Only when he left just as casually as he came in did the laughter die down. He returned, his eyes dancing with amusement and a big grin on his face.

For several years, Michael and Jeanne belonged to a supper club that met several times a month. There was always a lot of liquor consumed at those get-togethers and on one particular night, the drinks were flowing heavily. Feeling in a wild and playful mood, Michael disappeared, and Jeanne wondered where he had gone. Moments later, he returned dressed in only the hostess's two-piece bikini bathing suit, repeating the surprise he had tried at a previous party. It stopped the party cold as everyone's mouth fell open watching Michael modeling the suit, walking around among his friends as if he always wore a woman's bathing suit to parties. The raucous laughter, whistles and cat-calls could be heard all over the building. People had tears running down their cheeks they had laughed so hard. Michael loved it.

In the late summer of '65, Jeanne was at the restaurant enjoying her hostess role when Michael came over to her and asked her to sit down with him for a minute. Jeanne was surprised because he rarely even acknowledged her, much less spoke with her. Michael had tried to get Jeanne to have an affair, and he acknowledged his failed plans to her.

Insecurity, desperation, and a need to be loved were the real reasons that she started divorce proceedings.

But, before she went to a lawyer, Jeanne made arrangements to have another operation on her feet. She felt Michael owed her that much. It was a misguided action with the wrong intentions. She harbored such anger towards him and their marriage, she wanted to retaliate and get one last thing from him as payment for all the years she had suffered. The doctor at Johns Hopkins did a good job, but Jeanne's bitter spirit caused the result to be less than perfect.

During her hospital stay and the recovery time, she forced herself to take an honest look at the way she had been treating Michael and all the other men in her life after she read the book, Southern Ladies and Gentlemen by author Florence King. It was an eye opener for her and became her Bible for understanding all the devious ways she had learned growing up in the southern culture of her time. Things that she had been doing without even realizing needed to be cut out of her life. The book showed her how unfeeling, selfish, and manipulative her behavior had been since she could remember.

Although Michael used women, especially her, she used him and other men, too. There was no excuse for her behavior. She made herself a promise to change. But it was a difficult task she had given herself to fly in the face of her culture. Removing patterns of behavior that had been ingrained in her were almost impossible. Time and time again, she found herself reverting back to the more comfortable pattern, that of a typical, flirtatious, manipulative southern belle.

Jacksonville society's gossip was running riot with Michael's involvement with a woman who lived in Miami. After hearing about his current love, she did some soul searching. A small part of her still vacillated between wishing she could make Michael happy and wanting to leave him and find someone who she could love and who could love her. Was there someone else out there who she could have a real love affair with? She was tired of trying to understand and please Michael.

She began praying for someone to come into Michael's life that he would love and leave her alone. She made one mistake, however. She forgot to ask Spirit for a woman who would allow Michael to be a father to their three children.

Knowing that Jeanne was going to sue for divorce and the resultant turmoil, her mother, Nell, offered to send the boys to Admiral Farragut's Military Day School for the year. Neal was thirteen, in seventh grade and David was eleven, in fifth grade. Neal loved the order and discipline of the school, but Jeanne wasn't sure how David felt about it. He either wasn't able to express his feelings or wasn't sure what they were teaching being in that type of school. They were planning on attending the following year, but Nell decided not to pay for their schooling again. Neal went to Catholic high school and David returned to public school. The boys didn't do well in either.

Jeanne knew from several sources that Michael had hired the detective to follow her on her trip to see Mimi. She knew he wanted something on her to use in court and would have the detective testify.

During the divorce proceedings, to prove Michael was an alcoholic, she needed the testimony of her friends who had witnessed his alcoholic episodes for years. But not one would do it, so Jeanne subpoenaed all of them and made them stay outside waiting to be called each day of the hearings. She never called on them to testify, she just made them sit there. Michael threatened Jeanne that he would screw every woman who testified against him.

All their husbands had helped Michael get out of jail at various times for drunk driving, but they wouldn't help her either by swearing that Michael was an alcoholic. No fault divorce was not an option, it had not entered the judicial system, yet. If she couldn't prove he was an alcoholic, she wouldn't get her divorce.

In desperation, Jeanne subpoenaed her maid to testify because she was Jeanne's only hope to satisfy the court. Her maid had seen Michael dead drunk many times. As unfaithful as Michael was, he didn't want Jeanne to divorce him. It would cost him child support and alimony. Being married also made his public image look good. To that end, Michael had talked to their maid and blackened Jeanne's name by suggesting that Jeanne was very interested in a man named Pete and Michael was a wronged husband, hoping to sway her testimony.

In court the judge ordered, "Now, Ormay, you tell me about Mr. Corrigan's alcoholism. How did you know he was drunk?"

"Well, your honor, he took one step forward and two steps backwards," Ormay stated which helped Jeanne's case.

To present an image that would win the judge's approval, Jeanne wore her hair in pig tails, had on a long dress and her sturdy brogans on her feet. She sat as far away from the judge as she could. He would ask her a question and she would say, "Yes, your honor," very softly. She wanted the judge to feel sorry for her.

The judge misinterpreted her quiet answers as embarrassment and said, "Sweetie, I can't hear you. Why don't you come here and sit next to me."

Before the case, Jeanne had read an article slanted towards men that the judge had written, stating his views about why men shouldn't pay alimony. However, to his credit in court, he was a fair judge and believed Jeanne's testimony as to Michael's alcoholism. He was so moved he laid into Michael so hard, Michael's temper got the best of him and he stood up menacingly.

The judge said, "You take one step towards me and I'll push this button and you'll be in jail in a minute." So Michael sat down.

The judge went on and said, "I have no proof of any income except for two thousand dollars. "

Jeanne had kept records for five years on every dime they had spent in the Green Derby, getting prepared for the divorce, but the judge said he couldn't accept them. He did say, however, "I know for a fact, Mr. Corrigan that you have spent over two hundred thousand dollars a year for the past few years. You have trips to Los Vegas, and have huge expenses that are listed as business related that are ridiculous. You rarely pay your bills, but I can't do anything about that. All I can award you, Mrs. Corrigan is a thousand dollars for all those years with your husband and a thousand dollars goes to your ex-husband."

In a bitter tone, Michael said, after it was all over, "I'm going to ruin you because of this divorce and send you home to your mother."

"Michael, you haven't been happy with our marriage since the very first. I felt sometimes you wanted to be married and sometimes, you didn't. I never knew what you wanted. Even now, I don't know if you are sad or happy about it now that it's happened. If you remember, you asked me for the divorce.',

When Michael didn't reply, but turned and walked away, Jeanne still didn't know how he felt and wondered if he didn't know how he really felt, either. It was damned if she did and damned if she didn't when she was getting the divorce. What a bittersweet ending. In Jeanne's heart, knew her prayers to Spirit had been answered. She had asked Spirit, repeatedly to have Michael ask her for the divorce because she knew he was as miserable as she was. Spirit had given her, her wish. Later, she realized she had made a big mistake. She had not asked Spirit to give Michael a wife who would accept and welcome her children into their home so they could see their father on a regular basis.

Michael was ordered to pay Jeanne alimony and child support, but after the first month's payment, he never paid her even one dime more. He also went back to court and claimed that he had no income the following year. That was Jeanne's God-fearing Catholic ex-husband.

After they signed the papers in June 1970, Jeanne's life was still intertwined with Michael because of their children. The gossipers had a field day when they found out Michael had remarried. Jeanne refused to discuss the whole sordid mess with her friends knowing it would hurt her children in the long run and that was one thing she wanted to avoid at all costs. Michael was her children's father, and she knew they loved him no matter what he did.

Michael's new wife, Carol, made it very difficult for the children to see Michael or allow him to include them in his life. Beside herself, Jeanne went to confront her one day as a last resort.

Standing at the front door, when Carol opened it, Jeanne held nothing back and asked, "I want to ask you why you won't let Michael see his children? They have tried repeatedly to talk to him and you have stopped every attempt they have made."

"I will not discuss my life with Michael with you. I have my own children to consider and that's all I'm going to say about it." She closed the door and left Jeanne standing there, furious and unable to do anything about it. Because of Michael's new wife, his children felt cut off from him and consequently grieved for him the rest of their lives.

If you don't know where you are going, any road will get you there. Lewis Carroll

5. ONE REBOUND AFTER ANOTHER

1970 - 1975

JEANNE

Two days after her divorce was final, Jeanne went to see her old Cathedral roommate Mimi at Block Island. Mimi was despondent about her marriage and wanted a divorce like Jeanne got. Jeanne gave Mimi some of her traveler's checks and said, "Whenever you are ready and want to come and stay with me, come. Here's the means to do it."

She and Mimi had planned to celebrate her freedom by taking a trip to New England. They spent two wonderful weeks, together. They had been apart for such a long time that they enjoyed every intimate moment they had together. It was the most heavenly trip Jeanne had ever taken. They traveled all over New Hampshire and Vermont and Maine. From there they went to upper-state New York. It was August and some of the trees were beginning to change color. They drove through a beautiful forest. In the middle of it was a huge tree with its leaves turning golden. That tree told Jeanne that her world was good, and she and Mimi were always going to be together.

When the two weeks were over, Jeanne had to return to Jacksonville. It was always the same with her feeling desolate and alone.

It was hard to resume her responsibilities because she

had to face the fact: she was broke. How was she going to take care of three children? She thought, frantically. Searching her mind as to where she could find some fast money she remembered the engagement ring Michael had given her and what he had said when he gave it to her. He had lovingly teased her as he slipped the huge diamond on her finger, and said, "Now, everyone will know who you belong to."

She swallowed her pride, tucked her ring safely in her purse and went looking for him. She hadn't planned on her angry outburst when she found him, but she had been hurt and thoughts of their miserable life together surfaced, quickly.

Standing, facing him, she said, "I didn't want to come, Michael, but I'm broke. I can overlook the fact you haven't paid me any alimony, but you haven't given me any money for your three children! Don't you have any conscious about that?"

She took her ring out of her purse and asked, "Remember what you said to me when you gave it to me about belonging to you. Well, now, everyone will know who I don't belong to. Take your ring and give me the money for it. I'm trying to take care of your three children.

Surprising her, for whatever guilty reason he might have had, Michael agreed. "I'll have the money for you in a day or so and he did.

Satisfied, that she could at least pay for groceries and rent for a while, she knew she had to do something quickly to take care of her predicament. With no immediate way to support herself; no alimony or child support from Michael who ignored his court ordered obligations, Jeanne needed a wealthy husband.

Almost as if it were planned, she received a long distance call from Joe Steadman. He had been a young naval cadet she met when she was in high school at the Cathedral. She remembered him fondly, knowing how infatuated he was with her when she had flirted, teased and danced with him at the tea dances at Annapolis. She hadn't thought about him in years, but there he was in her life again.

"I'm so glad to talk to you, again. I called your high school, and they gave me your number and address." he said. "I'd like to come see you. Are you married or anything?"

"I'm definitely not married. I just got a divorce, but I have three kids, two boys and a girl."

"I'm divorced, too, and have four kids," he replied. "So, we have a lot in common." He paused momentarily, and said, before Jeanne could reply, "Your voice is just like I remembered it. I bet you're just as pretty as you were in high school. As for me, I'm in pretty good shape. I work-out and ride a bike."

Jeanne soon tuned him out because he kept talking non-stop about himself and his life. When he was quiet for a moment, she said, "Why don't you come and visit. Just let me know when."

"How about next week? I'm dying to see you." He proceeded to carry on a monologue until she interrupted again and said, "I have to go now, I'm late for an appointment. See you in a week," and hung-up.

Although he talked a lot, she thanked Spirit for helping her by sending Joe. Perhaps, he would be someone who could help her through the rough time she was feeling.

Joe wasn't aware, but he turned her friends off when he came to visit because of his continual banter. They called Jeanne and told her so. But Jeanne thought my friends can afford to be picky. They are not broke with a family to take care of. I was married to Michael who never talked and had affairs. Even though Joe talks a lot, perhaps I can stand to listen if he's paying the bills. I don 't care what my friends think, Joe's well off and that's important.

She could tell almost the moment she met Joe that he

was in love with her. She wasn't, but perhaps she could learn to love him. It wasn't long before Joe impetuously asked her to marry him. She ignored her friends' advice, didn't listen to her intuition that warned her of her foolish decision and agreed.

But the night before the wedding, at a candlelight dinner, he seemed edgy and overly talkative. As the evening wore on, he finally said, "Jeanne, I haven't been honest with you about my finances. I've been paying alimony, have my four children to take care of and the money just seems to disappear. I don't have any savings, but I do have a good job with NASA in Colorado and will make plenty of money, enough to take care of our big family."

Upset over his confession, which destroyed any plans she might have had of living a more comfortable life, Jeanne wanted to back out, but couldn't stand to tell her family or friends that she had made a mistake. The embarrassment would be too great. All the arrangements had been made and her family and friends were coming to Tampa from Jacksonville to celebrate with her.

When she said good night to Joe that night, she didn't sleep much thinking about what she had gotten herself into trying to provide for her children and herself. What was I thinking? Marrying a man with four children and my three, I will be in charge in charge of seven children! How will they all get along? Why had I panicked and said yes?

But the following morning, she stood tired and uncomfortably next to Joe as the minister pronounced them man and wife. Part of her discomfort was physical. She was recovering from the foot surgery paid for by Michael. Instead of being able to rest with her feet up, she was packing for Colorado where Joe had a well-paying job.

When they arrived in Colorado, problems between the two different families began immediately. Both sets of children became enemies with each other. There was continued fighting for the most favorable position in the integrated family. Jeanne became a referee, settling quarrels, trying to be fair, but not enjoying dealing with Joe's kids. She didn't know them and thought they were rude and disagreeable. They accused her of playing favorites and didn't like her. Mary Ann was very unhappy in that menagerie and her boys were always defending themselves.

Trying to integrate two families into one proved to be beyond Jeanne's patience and endurance. Her sore and painful feet rebelled and caused her so much agony, that many nights she had to crawl up the stairs, unable to walk. One night, at her wits end, she got down on her knees and prayed to Spirit, saying," I can't do this anymore. I have to leave for my children's sakes and my sanity."

Once she made up her mind, she secretly began making plans by opening a private bank account and depositing funds into it each week. After a month or so, she had enough money to buy plane tickets for her family and their dog. She had a meeting with everyone involved attending and told them what she was planning.

When Michael found out she was back, he stepped up and offered his apartment, rent free for her and the children. His generous offer gave Jeanne hope that they could be friends.

Once she was settled, she asked Joe for a divorce and offered him help with his problem with IRS, in return for giving her a divorce. Joe had filed a false income tax report, claiming her and her children as dependents after she had left.

Jeanne said, "Don't worry, I knew a judge who can help you. He was a lawyer for the IRS before he became a judge and knows the ropes." She didn't mention the fact that she was dating the judge at the time.

Being a good guy who was so grateful not to face some serious consequences with the IRS, he sent her some money that was part of the settlement with the government. Thanking her for helping him out of a bad situation, he said he had no bad feelings towards her and wished her well. He was a gentleman, even if he talked too much.

Jeanne thanked Spirit for bringing the judge into her life to help Joe and in doing so helped her, financially. It seemed that she was always taken care of when she needed it most.

One day, Michael called her and said, "I'm sorry that I have to tell you, but I had to sell the apartment for financial reasons."

"I understand, Michael. I think my mother will give me rent money so I can stay in this area. You have been very generous letting us live here for as long as you have."

Michael paused and asked, "Jeanne, I was wondering if you would be willing to throw a party for me at the apartment before you left? You always threw a great party. I owe a few favors."

Jeanne was surprised at his request, but she wanted to repay him for his generosity and said, "Sure, Michael, I have friends that can help me."

Jeanne called her friend, Kate, who was a gourmet chef, to see if she and her husband could help her. They agreed, came, and produced a table full of delicious canapés and desserts. Michael supplied the wine, beer, and liquor and together everything was ready when his guests arrived.

The guest were mostly men, dark haired with swarthy complexions. Jeanne watched them, turned to Kate and said, "The guests look like Mafia." Two minutes later, a tall, blond-haired man came in and Jeanne said, "He's FBI." "How do you know?" Kate whispered.

I just do, it's a gift I have."

"Do the other men know who he is?"

"No, of course not, I just know, that's all."

There were many beach volleyball games played on the beach that night, including the blond agent. Her children joined in the fun which was a mistake because Jeanne learned that that FBI agent had put her innocent children's names on file, along with all the Mafia after the party.

During the evening, Michael found Jeanne and said, "Great party, I'd like you to meet someone very special," She followed him downstairs to a big black car parked in the garage where he introduced her to a little, dark complected man by saying, "I want you to meet the God father, Jeanne." She wasn't impressed. She knew he and Michael were friends, but he had no place in her life.

A few days later, before Jeanne moved out to a nearby area on the beach, Mary Ann had run away, again. Jeanne immediately began making inquiries through Michael and others as to where Mary Ann might have gone. She didn't want to report her missing because Michael told her unhappily that the FBI had Mary Ann's name on file.

When Jeanne came back from Colorado, she had immediately enrolled in a date programming class to find a way to support herself and her children. She reluctantly returned to it one morning in spite of her intuition sending her urgent warnings about her daughter. Mary Ann was out there alone and didn't know where her mother had moved. Jeanne agonized about going but knew she couldn't miss any more classes and graduate.

Jeanne's new rental on the beach had the FBI on one side and a drug dealer on the other. The FBI agents were guarding David Eisenhower and his wife who also lived on the beach and the drug dealer was selling drugs.

It wasn't the first time that Jeanne had been faced with Mary Ann's running. When Jeanne and family lived in Colorado, Mary Ann at age thirteen had a girl friend who had helped her steal a car in Colorado so they could go to Florida.

Frantic to find her, Jeanne had received a call from a jail in Cheyenne, Wyoming from the sheriff to come get her daughter. It seemed the girls thought they were driving south but were really driving west. At thirteen, they couldn't read maps very well. The following morning when Jeanne tried to start one of their two cars to go get Mary Ann, it was 40 below zero and both cars were frozen solid.

A day later, in a rental car, Jeanne was finally able to go and rescue the two adventurers. When she arrived at the jail and they were released in her custody, Mary Ann told her mother how much fun she had had in jail. "My innocent, silly daughter, Jeanne thought as she took the girls to a hotel. When they were fed and safe in the hotel, Jeanne began questioning Mary Ann about the real reason she ran away.

Mary Ann became very quiet and said, "Joe's son started offering me drugs the minute we got there. I took some for fun and liked how they made me feel. Then he started to want some physical stuff from me to pay for the drugs. But the worst thing that happened was your creepy husband who began trying to touch me when no one was around. That really bummed me out and my girlfriend and I decided to run to Florida. I was going to ask Grandmother to take us in." That was when Jeanne knew she had to leave as soon as possible and she did.

Another bad decision, Jeanne thought. I married him for all the wrong reasons, knew it before I did it and did it anyway. When am I going to follow my intuition? I took the easy way out instead of standing on my own two feet. I guess I was tired of being broke.

Working for a living was something her mother had always frowned on, but Jeanne wanted her independence and rebelled against the way she had been raised to believe Southern ladies did not work. The world was changing and it was time for Jeanne to find her way. Only wealthy women like her mother had the privilege of living in the old fashioned style of never working outside the home. Jeanne, unfortunately, while being raised as a child like she was wealthy, didn't have a trust fund to fall back on during bad marriages and divorces.

At her data processing course, one morning, Jeanne's intuition was screaming that she had to leave, immediately because of Mary Ann. She rushed to the front of the room, gave a quick excuse to the teacher about a family emergency and drove back to Jacksonville Beach like a bat out of hell. She leaped out of her car and hurried next door to ask for help from her drug dealing neighbor. Unfortunately, he was gone and his wife answered the door.

Jeanne blurted out, "I'm going to the half-way house to find my daughter. Tell your husband if I'm not back by six o'clock to call the police and tell them where I went."

Jeanne shuddered when she drove up to the half-way house, a polite name for the dump where the kids hung-out before they were sent to California to be used as prostitutes. Fortunately, the door was open, so the guy there couldn't stop her. Looking wildly around, Jeanne spotted one of Mary Ann's awful girlfriends, a short, fat child with the nasty mouth of a long shore-man.

Jeanne gave her a bone chilling look and said, "I want Mary Ann and I want her now!"

The nasty mouthed girl snapped back, "You're not going to get her."

That was the wrong thing to say to Jeanne and she picked up the little 'smart-aleck' with one hand, slammed her against the wall and began pushing on her fat little body: Hard. "You tell me where my daughter is now, or you will live to regret it."

The girl's eyes got wide and with a terrified look on her face she led Jeanne to Mary Ann. Clutching her daughter with a death grip, Jeanne started out into the hall. Suddenly, her next door neighbor was next to her and whispering, "I want you to stay right with me. Do not do or say anything." He put an arm around Mary Ann on one side of him and Jeanne walked next to him on the other, slowly out the door. Jeanne saw three men lying on the floor that he had evidently knocked-out when he came in to keep them from killing the three of them.

After guiding them to safety and the beach rental, her neighbor left them safe and sound.

Jeanne thanked him over and over, then took her daughter into their house and put her to bed. Jeanne sat there in the dark, going over the frightening experience she and Mary Ann had just gone through and wondered how much more was in store for either or both of them. She knew she had to report Mary Ann who was on probation with the FBI for stealing a car and when she finally called, she was told she had to send Mary Ann to a half-way house for drug rehabilitation. Sick at heart that her beautiful, young daughter had to be taken from her and sent to a rehab program, Jeanne promised herself that she would help Mary Ann in every way possible, once she was out. Little did Jeanne know that Mary Ann was to meet her future husband who was a drug counselor in the program.

It was a sobering feeling to know that her sweet girl was mixed up in drugs and had to go away to a rehab program. How had all of this happened? Things seemed more out of control more than ever. Her two boys were growing up and could also become drug addicts. Neal was twelve and David, ten. She asked Spirit to watch over them all and help her keep them away from drugs.

Determined, Jeanne went back to Jacksonville to complete her course. She stopped renting the beach house because of the drug scene, moved in with her friend, Kathy and put her boys safely with the grandmothers while she finished school and graduated.

Thanks to her mother's contacts, she landed a good position in a St. Petersburg bank. With Jeanne secure in a job, her mother offered to buy her a house, but Jeanne turned her down.

Jeanne said, "In six months, you will ask me to assume the house payments because you will say you can't continue to pay them. I won't be able to afford the payments on a fancy house. I'm going to rent a place. It won't be in the best part of town, but I will be able to afford it.

Her mother threatened her by saying, "Jeanne, if you don't let me buy you a house, I won't pay any of your other bills. You'll be strictly on your own. Why would you ever think that I would ask you to pay for the house payments after six months, that's preposterous?"

Jeanne knew it would be a stretch for her to keep current with her always enlarging number of bills because of her children, so she agreed, reluctantly to her mother's terms. Things were not going well for her besides. Her bank job was rife with politics and intrigue that she couldn't handle.

Try as she might, she was lonely. Her house was almost empty and immediately she thought about finding another man. Only he could take that awful feeling away. The next thing she knew she had planned a trip to Ashville NC to find him. She had been thinking about him off and on for months. She had to see him. To sweeten the trip, Jeanne had come into a little windfall from her family. She had sold a piece of property and had a small nest egg to finance her new life.

Once there, she impetuously rented an apartment in Ashville NC and enrolled in a school to pursue her interest in data processing. The field was wide open, growing and changing all the time and she wanted to be in on the innovations taking place.

Her children were almost grown. Mary Ann was married. Neal was out of school and self-employed, and David was in his senior year of high school. He had a friend, Mike, who he spent a lot of time with, almost lived with his family and planned on staying with him while Jeanne was visiting and making her plans to find a new man.

Having spent the day finding a place to rent and enrolling in school, she met a new man named Archie for lunch and they spent the time together being so excited with her move. She had been there for two or three days when Archie invited her out for dinner at a lovely restaurant. She knew something was wrong when she explained more about her plans for moving there and his response was not very positive.

After dinner, she asked bluntly, "Do you want me to leave or stay?"

Archie looked at her for the longest time and finally said, softly, "I can't handle it."

At the moment, Jeanne's chest hurt she felt so crushed. All of her plans to be with him were gone. What had she been thinking about? Things would never be the way she had imagined they would be with Archie. Had she been living in a fantasy world as far as Archie was concerned? She had made a big mistake by invading his territory. It forced him to decide whether he wanted to live with her or stay as he was. Down deep, she knew it was the beginning of the end of her dreams with him, but she knew in her heart that it was the best thing for him. However, it didn't make it any easier.

She left, hurt and returned to St. Petersburg to her lonely life, sad, but resigned. She told herself it was all for the best, but that didn't take the ache away.

Six months to almost the day, her mother and some friends came to see Jeanne and her mother said she was in financial difficulty and asked Jeanne to assume her own house payments.

"Mother, Spirit told me you would do that and you have. I find myself in a position of not having enough money to deal with all the problems in my life. I know Spirit wants me to learn to stand on my own two feet and take care of my finances which I am trying to do as hard as it is, but I just barely meet my expenses with the kids each month and can't assume the payments. You have no idea what it's like to be a single parent. Mary Ann's expenses at the rehab center, the boy's clothes and food take every bit of money I have. Michael was supposed to pay for Mary Ann's rehab but hasn't sent me a dime for it. He knows I'm too strapped financially to go back and hire a lawyer to petition the court to force him to pay me what he should, and he is counting on that."

To make himself feel less guilty, Michael came to visit Mary Ann periodically and brought a lot of money with him to spend generously on all of them, especially during the holidays. He never gave Jeanne any of it, however. He never admitted it, but he hadn't gotten over his divorce from Jeanne.

One Christmas, he had said he was coming to see them all, and Jeanne immediately bought a lot of nice Christmas presents for the family and for him, putting them all on lay away. At the last moment, he cancelled and said he was going skiing with a woman named Carol. He married her not long after that.

To add to her worries, Jeanne's old roommate, Mimi, called Jeanne one evening, and said, "Chrissie and I need a place to stay. You invited me to come when I saw you on your trip. I just got my divorce and I'm broke."

"Of course, you must come. My place is small, but I can squeeze you in." Jeanne didn't know how she would do it, but she didn't have the heart not to offer her best friend from high school a place to stay.

"I'm so grateful, Jeanne. I've been at my wit's end,"

"Friends take care of friends. It's a hard world out there. I know from experience."

Jeanne drove to get them and took them in, making them feel very welcome.

With Mary Ann in rehab, Jeanne took every chance she could to visit Mary Ann, went to some of the parties they had at the center and was a concerned mother.

On one visit, Mary Ann seemed preoccupied and nervous when Jeanne got there. After a little while, Jeanne asked, "What's wrong, Mary Ann?"

"Mom, I don't know how to tell you this, but I'm going to have a baby. Its father is a counselor here. We're in love and I don't know what to do."

"Uh, well, how are you feeling and how far along are you?" Jeanne asked, hugging her daughter and trying not to show her surprise or concern.

"Not too far and I feel okay, but not great."

"I'll see about having you come home to have your baby and talk to the administrator. It may take a while because of all the red tape."

"I'll be waiting, Mom. Please come back, soon."

"I will, honey, don't worry," Jeanne replied, sounding more positive than she felt with her fifteen-year-old daughter's pregnancy.

Mary Ann had a miscarriage the following month and didn't have any real reason to leave, but six months later, she told her mother she was pregnant again. "Mom, Jan and I love each other and want to get married," she said, softly.

"This time I'm going to make sure you can leave without the administrator stalling."

Jeanne said, "I'll go see that person, now, and get the necessary papers signed."

When Jeanne spoke to the director of the program and explained the reason, she wanted Mary Ann to come home, the administrator said, "You owe us for the time Mary Ann has been with us and I can't let you leave without paying."

"I set it up for my ex-husband, Michael to pay Mary Ann's expenses. Didn't he pay?"

"He never contacted us and hasn't paid anything. So, the bill is yours."

"Did you tell him he was responsible?"

"We never talked," the woman replied.

"That's too bad because you aren't getting any money from me. You were in charge when my daughter got pregnant and evidently weren't supervising these young people." Jeanne packed Mary Ann's clothes and walked her out to the car. Jan arrived soon after, they squeezed into Jeanne's tiny house and Jan looked for a job while Jeanne and Mary Ann prepared for the wedding.

Jeanne had many moments when she thought about her daughter's future. These kids are just a couple of kids themselves. She's 16 and he's 17. They are getting married and having another kid. How will they make it?

When the wedding date and the church was rented, Jeanne called Michael and said, "Hi, Father of the bride, I wanted to invite you to your daughter's wedding on............date, and ask you if you would walk her down the aisle? I also would like you to supply the liquor for the party I'm having afterwards at my house. It would help me a lot because my money is hard to come by."

"Sure, I can bring the liquor and I'm very happy to walk my daughter down the aisle. I can't believe she's old enough to get married. Time really gets away from me, sometimes."

"She isn't, but she's pregnant. She's only a couple of years younger when WE had to get married." Jeanne said, having a nostalgic moment.

On the day of the wedding, Mary Ann was on pins and needles in the back of the church waiting for her dad to come. The minutes ticked by. He finally whirled in a half an hour late with his bodyguard and ran into the grateful arms of his daughter who was watching for him.

"Dad, you made it. I was so worried you might have forgotten."

"Honey, I would never forget your wedding. You look beautiful? Let's go," he said, taking her arm and starting down the aisle in step with the music.

Their wedding was a simple, sweet, and unpretentious affair. It was all Jeanne could afford.

At Jeanne's house, with Michael's liquor, the party went into full swing. Michael had been drinking steadily during the day from emotion. Jeanne watched him go outside to the back yard where he stood for a while. The next time she looked, Michael was on the trampoline and beginning to jump. Most of the other male guests were fifteen or twenty years younger than he was. He was having trouble with his balance, perhaps because of his inebriated state. She thought he had already lost his good judgment by even getting on the trampoline.

As Michael jumped higher and higher enjoying himself immensely, he lost his balance, fell off the trampoline into the grass and broke his shoulder. She watched his bodyguard help him into their car. Later, she found out he spent the rest of the afternoon in the hospital being x-rayed and having a shoulder cast put on. Back at the party, no one except Jeanne noticed he was gone.

With no means to afford a place of their own, much less the groceries, it had been decided before the wedding that Mary Ann and Jan would continue to live with Jeanne. Consequently, their little house was full to overflowing with Mimi and her daughter, Chrissie still living there. Jeanne slept on the porch, and her guests had the bedrooms.

It wasn't long before everything changed, however. Mimi and Chrissie moved into their own place; Mary Ann had her baby boy: Sonny. Jan got a job. Both he and Mary Ann were drug free, in love, and things were looking up except Jeanne was lonely.

With no special man in her life, Jeanne's thoughts turned to her data processing teacher, Robert -*Phillips. He had showed a lot of interest in her when she was his student, was single and seemed like a nice guy. She thought I could use his help with my new job, and it would be a perfect way to get to know him.

When she contacted him, he seemed delighted and willingly offered her assistance.

Pleased with his response, she thanked him and said she was looking forward to seeing him, again. It was pleasant working with him, and they became friends. One afternoon, Rob asked her out for dinner and after that they began seeing each other, more and more after work. One thing led to another, and she knew Rob was very interested in her and she wondered what she would do if Rob asked her to marry him. She found him very intelligent, attractive, had good conversations with him and generally felt at ease with him. He popped the question in early December 1974, and she agreed. She had no idea that she had just leapt from the frying pan into the fire.

The day they were to go for their marriage license, Rob, exploded in a paranoiac attack on her boss, Frank, and accused him of flirting with his soon-to-be-wife because he had taken Jeanne out for lunch as a gesture of good will and a parting gift for her upcoming marriage to Rob.

At that moment, Jeanne wondered, Am I making another mistake? Her intuition was screaming at her to think about what she was doing, but she didn't listen. She listened, instead, to her soon-to-be husband as he threatened her boss by saying, "I don't ever want this to happen again, or you'll be sorry."

Jeanne's boss acted dumbfounded. Her intuition had continually warned her, strongly, not to marry him, but she ignored the advice. She didn't question her decision even after watching her fiancé out of control. But it wasn't long before Rob's real personality began surfacing. Saying that he wanted to take care of her, he told her she had to stop working, immediately. Little by little he set up systematic controls over her, first in small ways, but soon his demands escalated and became obsessive. She began to feel like a prisoner in her own home.

During this time, Mary Ann brought Sonny to Neal to take care of while she went to Puerto Rico to buy drugs. Neal asked Jeanne to help him take care of Sonny because he had to work and also wanted to date a little. Jeanne loved seeing Sonny and they had lots of fun together. He was just a little over a year old and was fascinated with all kinds of little bugs, like all little children. But Jeanne was shocked when she attempted to bathe him. He screamed and acted terrified of the water. She was sure, he had been abused some way when that happened.

She didn't say anything to Neal when he came to take Sonny back with him, but she was worried. A few days later, Neal was driving with Sonny and had a bad wreck. Sonny was not hurt, although Neal was. When Jeanne went to the hospital to get the baby, Rob said that he would not be responsible for Neal's bills.

Jeanne called Jan and told him that Neal had been in a wreck, Sonny was okay and she was caring for him. When Jan came to get the baby, Jeanne told him about her concerns with Sonny's behavior in the bathtub. Jan said that that was the final straw, and he was going to divorce Mary Ann and get custody of Sonny.

Jeanne didn't let on about her own miserable marriage to Rob. He had enough trouble to deal with. She felt sorry for all of them, herself, Mary Ann, Jan and the baby, but she couldn't change what was happening. Feeling totally powerless, Jeanne allowed Rob to victimize her in almost the same way she had been treated as a youngster by her mother. It was a pattern in her life, allowing people to take advantage of her. Her mother had dictated what she could and couldn't do in the most uncaring and unfeeling way. She had allowed him to cut her off from her family, friends from the past and her current bank friends. He had insisted that Mimi move out and the worst thing of all was his insistence that she only go to his doctor and not see her own doctor anymore. Little by little, she reverted back feeling child-like most of the time. All of her braveness and rebellious courage had disappeared.

One evening after they were married, Jeanne was preparing dinner and Rob was in the kitchen with her, very angry about a work-related incident. He picked a fight, as usual, and she could see he was getting madder and madder. He got up quickly and moved toward her, aggressively. She thought he was getting ready to attack her. She quickly remembered a small, but important bit of information about him that he had admitted to her when they were dating. He was terribly afraid of knives of any kind.

"You take one step closer to me and I will kill you," she yelled at him, grabbing a kitchen knife, and pointing it at him. I have an onion in my other hand, and I can kill you or cut up this onion with the knife." When she threw those insane words at him, she knew she was sick and needed help.

Desperate, she asked Rob to allow her to go see his doctor and he agreed.

She made an appointment and the day she was to go she was nervous, but determined to find out what was the matter with her. When the nurse called her into the doctor's office, she felt relieved to be able to tell him how bad she felt.

"Doctor, I came to see you because I feel completely disoriented and strange. " I don't know what's wrong with me. I feel as if you were to cut me open, every nerve in my body would be jumping."

The doctor replied, seriously, "You are having a nervous

breakdown." He dashed off a prescription and said, "Take three Lithium pills three times a day. They will make you feel less jumpy and nervous. Come back in a week and let me know if you feel any better."

He also said, Mrs. Henderson, I've been treating your husband for years and I'm concerned about your safety. Rob is a sick man, but he refuses to go for help. I personally think he is a paranoid schizophrenic and is capable of doing you bodily harm. Until you make up your mind to leave, take my advice and don't argue with him."

"I'm feeling terrible and all you can do for me is give me pills and suggest I leave?" Isn't there anything else you can do?

"No, I'm giving you good advice. I can't commit him until he does something to give me a reason. I don't want you to be the reason. Pick a time when he isn't around and run. Go to your family, friends, anywhere, but get out of that house.',

Distraught with her life, Jeanne struggled to get to the drug store, picked up her prescription and went home in a terrible depression. Each time she popped her handful of pills into her mouth, she felt that her body and mind were breaking down. She was taking meds for her ulcer, her headaches and now for her nerves. While she waited for the medications to kick-in, she sat thinking about the advice the doctor had given her. She finally had to face what she had felt all along. Rob was mentally ill, and she was really afraid for her life. What she needed was a strong friend and she didn't have one. Michael was remarried, Joe was in Colorado, Archie had chosen to stay separate from Jeanne and her father was dead.

She sunk lower into depression and confusion with the days and nights blending into a long nightmare for her. She had no fight left in her. She faithfully took her pills and slept a lot. Rob continued in his crazy, paranoid way, contributing to her breakdown by keeping her continually off balance with all of his crazy accusations. In a fury, he accused Jeanne of having an affair with his son. The final straw was him giving her car to her son, David, so he could deliver pizzas from the pizza parlor to the customers. She was completely under his control.

Desperate, she tried to commit suicide by drinking Canadian Club and coke all night and eating handfuls of pills. Instead of dying, she woke up feeling terrible the next day with the mother of all hangovers. Walking around the house in a drug induced daze, all she could hear was laughter coming from voices all around her. Putting her hands over her ears, she couldn't make them stop until she got down on her knees and said weakly over and over, "I surrender, I can't do anything else, I just surrender." She laid down on the sofa and fell into a deep sleep. When she awoke, her mind was clearer than it had been in months and she knew what she had to do, but she felt paralyzed to do it.

Rob, in his sick way, asked Jeanne for a divorce at least once a month. She knew he was testing her. If she agreed she was afraid he might kill her. He was a ticking time-bomb. Part of her was terrified of him, part of her hated him.

One night, she knew he was building up to something. He came home from work in a rage.

An hour later, he walked into the kitchen where she was attempting to cook and said, "I want a divorce, now.

She shuddered and said, carefully, "Okay," hanging onto the kitchen counter, feeling weak in the knees. He fooled her and didn't react in a rage, but he was so calm he was scary. He packed up and left, silently, taking his belongings and her antique dresser with him. He obviously had found another place to live. She held her breath until he was out of her house thinking at any moment he would explode, but he didn't. She relaxed a little but had a premonition that she had not heard the last of Rob.

To for-stall any future confrontations over money, she went to the bank for money to repay him for any extra expenses he might have incurred while they were living together.

Surprising her one morning, Rob returned unannounced in an ominous mood. Still trying to recover from living with him, Jeanne was tense and watchful, was ready to run if he tried to accost her.

He said angrily, "Since I've known you, I have spent all my money on you and you have ruined me, financially."

"I knew you'd be back making these accusations. But to make things right between us, I went to the bank for money to repay you for David's dirt bike, and my groceries. I've kept records since we were married in case you question me." She showed him her notebook, gave him the money to cover everything and said, "Now, get out of my house." She felt like a giant stone had been lifted off of her chest when he stalked out of the house.

Jeanne immediately called Mimi, told her the good news and asked her to come over. She needed to talk.

Mimi came over that afternoon to see Jeanne. As she confessed how awful she had felt since marrying Rob, he surprised them having coffee. Looking wild eyed and acting crazy, he grabbed Jeanne and said, "You're coming with me." He wrapped his arms around her and dragged her out of her house. She began kicking and screaming. Terrified, self-preservation became paramount to her. Outside, she fought back, struggling with him and screaming for the neighbors to help her and call her doctor. Jeanne knew she was on the edge of coming apart, and Rob was sending her over the edge. In desperation, she sat down on the sidewalk outside of their house. As he attempted to pick her up, Mimi waded-in to help her, steamed-up over the treatment Rob was dishing out to her friend. Rob shoved her down hard on the ground. Mimi felt dazed. Then the neighbors came running out. Rob took off in the opposite direction. They helped her gently into their house and followed her wish to call her doctor. He asked them to take her to the hospital where he would meet her.

"Doctor, I'm feeling frantic and need to be admitted to a psyche ward. I'm terribly afraid of my soon to be ex-husband. He's crazy!" she screamed.

"Don't worry about your husband, there are big orderlies to keep him from getting anywhere near you," as he walked down the hall with her to that section of the hospital. "Are you sure you want this, Jeanne?"

"Yes," she said quietly. "I need to feel safe and know he can't get to me."

Once she had been admitted, he spoke to the resident psychiatrist about Jeanne. After talking with him, her doctor asked her, "Would you like to see your family?"

"Yes, but not today, tomorrow."

Unbeknownst to Jeanne, when Mary Ann found out where her mother was and the reason why she was there, she was so enraged, she asked her father to put out a contract on Rob with the Mafia.

The night nurse gave Jeanne some pills to help her sleep and after a refreshing, healing sleep for the first time in months, Jeanne's mind began to clear.

When the resident psychiatrist visited her the next morning, he asked, "How can I help you? "

Jeanne replied, "I recently tried to commit suicide, and I'm on a self-destructive path because of my crazy husband. I'm running away from him and myself. And you know what, doctor, I'm tired of running."

"Why did you choose to come here?"

"It was the only place I knew I would feel safe."

"Has that happened?"

"Yes, and I want help, so I don't try to commit suicide again and my husband doesn't try to kill me."

"We'll keep you for a couple of days and try to help you

with your life," the handsome, young doctor offered.

When Michael brought their children and came to visit her, the following day, she thought she was ready to see Michael. She had to deal with him in order to see her children. He didn't talk much, he let the kids chatter away. But then he told her that he had called her mother and told her that Jeanne was there, and he guessed he was to blame. And her mother had told him yes.

There was a moment or two when she wished Michael loved her and they were all together as a family, but the moment was fleeting.

Michael also said, "Mary Ann called me in a panic, begging me to get in touch with the Mafia and put a contract out on Rob. I didn't do that, Jeanne. It wasn't a good idea."

"Mary Ann, I'm okay and I wouldn't ever want to cause anyone's death. It's not my right to do that. Only Spirit decides those things. I've had a bad time trying to live with Rob, but it's over now. I don't want you to worry about me. All I want is a divorce. When I get out of here in a couple of days, I'm going to file."

Michael looked at her in a thoughtful way. He was still as handsome as ever, but there were gray hairs creeping into that beautiful head of hair of his. She hated him most of the time for the unfeeling way he had treated her all those years they were married, but even with his infidelities, he wasn't a pervert like Joe or completely nuts like Rob.

Jeanne left after three days, feeling better than she had for some time. She had seen Michael and her children and her mother. Her mother had started to cry when she came to see Jeanne. For the first time in her life, Jeanne knew her mother felt guilty. She offered Jeanne her the condo on Long Boat Key to stay in as long as she needed until she recovered. Jeanne told her she was all right and not to feel bad. Jeanne didn't take any pleasure in making her mother feel any worse than she already felt.

When she had left the hospital, she had called Archie and he came to see her, immediately on Long Boat Key. He stayed three wonderful days and explained to Jeanne why he hadn't been able to see her in the hospital. Only family members or members of the clergy were allowed to see the patients in the psyche ward.

During her three days stay, crazy Rob and the chain of bizarre events living with him had catapulted her life in a new direction. She knew without a shadow of a doubt after spending many hours alone talking to Spirit asking for guidance, she knew she was given the task of changing the patterns in her life that were keeping her from her path.

Raised by her southern mother with the archaic rules of female behavior, Jeanne was determined to find a new and better way to live. She promised herself that she would learn to stand on her own, learn new ways of living, take care of her children and become a better person.

The journey of a thousand miles begins
with the first step. Lao Tzu

6. SEARCHING FOR ANSWERS

1975-1977

JEANNE

The minute Jeanne was discharged from the hospital she called Archie and asked him to visit her on Long Boat Key. Archie dropped everything and drove to see her.

Archie stayed for three glorious days. Having him there meant the world to her after the harrowing five months she had experienced living with a paranoid schizophrenic. He stabilized her, accepted her unconditionally and loved her with his whole heart. It was always the same with him and he completed her.

But something was better this time when they met because Jeanne had changed. She couldn't explain it to Archie or herself, but it had happened. It would take time to before she knew, but she was sure Spirit would lead her.

They spent more time in quiet solitude, walking the beach together as the sun was just peeping above the horizon and the day was beginning. It was then that they watched in awe the teeming life of shore birds, calling, flying and looking for their breakfasts. In the evening, they strolled more leisurely, holding hands as the dusky evening closed in around them the sun lost its heat and brilliance. As it dipped beneath the horizon, its final rays turned the clouds above into an array of dynamic reds, oranges and finally pink colors before the absent sun was completely gone. They walked until the sky was almost dark and didn't... That would come later.

Each evening, Archie took her out for wonderful dinners at quaint, local restaurants where they would eagerly share little intimate thoughts with each other over a glass of chilled wine. Their conversations were never planned, just enjoyed.

And afterwards, when they made love, Jeanne always knew when Archie was getting ready to say goodbye. He told her he loved her over and over, held her close to him and slept with his arms around her. His guilty conscience had begun its relentless drive to send him back to his chosen life of a gay man and she steeled herself for his departure.

Jeanne woke up the next morning after Archie left, lonely, her heart beating as if she had been running and seized with unknown fears. Having Archie there had forestalled them, but now they had invaded her. As her eyes flitted around her lovely bedroom, she thought, here I am in a beautiful condo on a beautiful beach, and I'm too scared to even move. I know I need to get over this, but I'm stuck. As she lay in bed desperate and grasping at straws, she thought, I'll make a list of everything I'm afraid of That's got to help! To stop them from running around in her head, in desperation she scribbled them down. After finishing her list, she read; I'm afraid to walk out my front door, I'm afraid of going to the grocery store, the drug store, or any other store, and then she hesitated. Her biggest fear was Rob, and she added, I'm afraid of Rob and him stalking me. I'm afraid of going to the beach in case he is hiding under a beach umbrella and jumps out trying to kidnap me. She began to shake just thinking about him.

But in her heart of hearts, she knew there was something missing. It wasn't good enough just to write them down, they were still there, laying-in- wait in her mind. She had to do more. She turned to Spirit and asked for help. Immediately, she received her answer, meditate.

As she wondered about that, another message concerning a Lutheran minister appeared like magic. She remembered a Lutheran minister who had talked about meditation and how good it was. It must be the way, she decided. It was difficult to leave the condo, but she struggled out to see him, excited to talk to him, but felt ambivalent about her session, afterwards. He had explained the technique and she had practiced it with limited success. She made two more appointments with him to refine what she had already learned.

She soon was able to look into her third eye in the center of her forehead, repeat a mantra as she breathed slowly in and out and begin to quiet her thinking mind. She knew she must clear her mind of all the little insignificant details and just be calm. That was the trick, but it would take practice like anything else.

After she had spent three sessions with him, she realized that she was the one asking her questions and answering them. The minister just sat there unable to do more for her. He had done what he was capable of, teaching her the way to meditate. Now, it was up to her to go into a special place and let Spirit talk to her. It felt right and calmed her body.

Now, she was ready to take each fear and meditate on it. Meditation opened her so she could receive help from Spirit to dissolve the fear. Spirit encouraged her to face her fear. When she did, it disappeared. She systematically did that every morning until suddenly, she woke up one day and realized her deepest fears were gone. She was no longer afraid and physically she didn't shake when she left the condo. It was a thrilling moment to know that she had conquered the fears and thanked Spirit for showing her the way. Filled with pride, Jeanne knew her life was changing for the better.

Mentally, she thanked the minister. He has served a bigger purpose for Jeanne. By only showing her the meditation technique and nothing else, he allowed her to discover her God given talent to heal. Her health had returned. It was a great awakening for her. Perhaps, she was meant to be a healer.

One of her favorite places to meditate was on the beach. The energy from the ocean, the gentle rhythmic sound of the waves, and the sun's vibrancy filled her with peace.

As peace filled her heart, she changed a pattern that she had clung to most of her life. She had believed that there was no way out of the situation, and she was stuck there without hope. But through meditation, opportunities and possibilities began appearing to her to solve her problems, allowing her choices and with them, more freedom.

As she healed, her attitude towards Rob took on a different perspective. He was the catalyst that propelled her to take a hard look at herself in the psyche ward. Those hours alone had made her question everything about her life.

The other positive outcome from her hospital stay was Michael's slight change in his attitude towards his part in her breakdown. When her mother came to see her, she told Jeanne that Michael had asked her if she thought he was to blame for Jeanne's illness. When she answered yes to his question, her mother said she thought he had admitted to a tiny bit of responsibility in how he had treated her daughter during their marriage.

David, who had been living with her, decided to leave and stay with Michael and Carol. As a wise mother, Jeanne didn't argue with him. She wanted him to experience Michael and his new wife and family. She knew as a teenager he wanted to get to know his father, again, which was normal, but she was afraid of the consequences. David lived with them for a year and returned suddenly. He never discussed why he came back or what happened at Michael's, but Jeanne knew David had found that his father had many sides to his personality and probably didn't like some of them. David had been suffering from depression and Jeanne knew his time with Michael hadn't alleviated it, but probably added to it.

Mary Ann was filtering in and out of Jeanne's life in the condo, too, after her divorce from Jan. She was going to beautician's school and one day, she announced, "My boyfriend, Juan from Puerto Rico is here." Jeanne was furious that Mary Ann had asked him to come and live with her at Jeanne's home without asking her.

Jeanne relented and he moved in, but soon Mary Ann got restless, had a fight with her boyfriend and left leaving Jeanne with Juan. One night, Jeanne went into his room and found a knife and a gun. When he came home, Jeanne asked him to sit down because she wanted to talk with him. She said, "You have twenty-four hours before you have to leave. Just tell me where you want to go and I'll send you there."

Juan said, "I want to go to New York City."

Jeanne put him on the plane, delighted he was gone.

As soon as Mary Ann found out he was gone, she came home, and Jeanne let her know that she didn't want anything like that to happen again.

One day, after a satisfying meditation on the beach, she aimlessly ran the sand through her fingers. As she did it, she thought, I will write down the name of every male I've ever been attracted too. She searched her brain for the names and as she thought about all of them, she saw similar patterns in their behavior. She wrote their names in the sand with her finger. With each one it became apparent that except for her father, all of them had had addictive personalities with leanings toward alcoholism. Most of them had been charming, handsome, and angry, including her father, but not Archie. For the rest, she asked, why have I been drawn to these kinds of men?

With that question unanswered in her mind, she turned to the biggest female nemesis in her life, her mother. All Jeanne's life she had been faced with Nell's obsessive, demanding personality, as her mother. Jeanne wondered did her life patterns start when she was in utero? Did she feel her mother's fear and unhappiness being pregnant? Did she suffer from her mother's anger having to drive herself back and forth from Lakeland to Tampa to see the only doctor she trusted?

Jeanne knew her mother's story well about how she suffered with phlebitis after her first baby, Nell Leigh, had been born. The same doctor had dedicated himself to making her well. But Jeanne had a lot of questions about her mother's pregnancy. Why didn't her father, Neal, drive her to see her doctor instead of working? Did she want another child? Nothing about the pregnancy was ever discussed. It was buried with a lot of other secrets in her mother's heart.

And then there was the trauma that Nell suffered in the car accident. Had her mother been driving too fast, angry about her pregnancy? Did she resent the long trips to see her doctor? Jeanne didn't know, but she did know without a shadow of a doubt that her inability to walk on slanted ground was directly related to the fear she felt in her mother's womb from her mother's terror as her car rolled over and over.

She listed all the positive and negative traits her mother had and realized that most of the men in her life had the same patterns. Michael, her first husband, was a prime example. He was a full-blown alcoholic. Was her mother a closet one, too? It was a stretch for Jeanne to think of her mother as one, but it seemed plausible and would explain a lot about her mother's unfair and abusive methods of punishing her when she was growing up.

Something else became clear to her after a long meditation. Her mother and Michael had the same patterns of manipulation and being very hurtful with no remorse. She had witnessed it time after time with both of them. Sometimes, it was directed towards her, but others suffered too. Neither one of them ever felt they had to apologize for any of their actions. Why had she chosen to deal with that kind of behavior? What was she supposed to learn? Was she at all like them? Children mimic what they see growing-up and she was a good mimic. It left her questioning a lot about who she really was and pushed her to make up her mind to find out. Perhaps, studying books in the field of psychology might help her.

Two books that made sense to her, immediately were: "I ain't much baby, but I'm all I got" and "I'm OK and You're OK." They allowed her to forgive herself. She also dabbled in some courses in Personal Psychology that made a lot of sense to her. But as she got further into the courses, she realized she couldn't practice as a counselor until she had a degree. That was out of the question, monetarily. She felt she had hit a brick wall and would never be able to live a meaningful life. It caused her to feel terribly depressed. She felt stuck again and needed to talk to Archie. She called Archie, crying, telling him her troubles.

He waited until she had finished and said, "I can't stay away, I've missed you so terribly since we last saw each other. Would you like me to come? Perhaps, I can help you."

"Yes, yes," she answered.

Jeanne immediately felt better with Archie there. He always had that effect on her, probably because he genuinely loved her. They spent three intimate days and nights together. The beach held a fascination for both of them and they spent hours there during the day, walking, swimming or just sitting quietly under an umbrella enjoying a cooling drink and breathing in the energy of the ocean.

The evenings felt like magic as they walked on the beach in the moonlight. It drew them back to the condo they surrendered to each other. Afterwards, when they shared their most personal thoughts with each other, one subject was never mentioned. It crept into Jeanne's mind and heart, uninvited and whispered, would she ever live with Archie? Down deep, she knew the answer, no. It would destroy Archie to leave his way of life. She loved him too much to ever let that happen. Three days later, Archie left. Their brief time together was over. Jeanne was alone again.

Spirit sent a friend's help in the form of a book to help her clearly understand her situation with Archie. It was called Wine and Music, The true story of a gay leaving the gay community to marry and the terrible times he and his wife had because of it. The gay ended up hating the woman he had married.

After reading the book, Jeanne knew she had made the right decision never to ask Archie to leave the gay community and live with her. She vowed to read that book every year after that and she did.

She would always carry Archie's love in her heart. Nothing would take that away from her. She would remember the way he showed his love for her, valued her opinions, and continually let her know how important she was to him. He was protective, tender, and caring, something she needed and would thank him for the rest of her life. She would never find a replacement for him, but perhaps she could find someone who had some of his magnificent qualities.

As time went on and she became more immersed in metaphysics and specifically astrology, she asked Archie if she could have his astrological chart done and he agreed. It validated her feelings about them not being together in this lifetime. She and he were triple flames and as such were fulfilling their commitments for this lifetime. Archie's soul was evolving in the masculine and hers, the feminine. If they continued on their present paths, in the next dimension when they were reunited as one, their soul's growth would move them to a higher vibrational level closer to Spirit. Knowing that helped Jeanne to dedicate her life to finding her way.

Although Jeanne still missed Archie, a wonderful thing occurred. Her childhood friend, Mary Alice, and Michael's sister, called her about a fantastic healer who was in town named Elmer Gans. She encouraged Jeanne to make an appointment with him for her feet. Mary Alice said several of her friends had given him glowing reports as far as his ability to heal.

Jeanne contacted him and made an appointment to meet with him. She had no idea how important that phone call was for her future. When she arrived, he calmly asked her to sit down and placed his hands on her feet. His hands got extremely warm, his face got very red and Jeanne's feet felt very good. He held his hands on her feet for ten minutes, removed them and said, "Stand up and push yourself up and down on your toes."

She was able to do it. It was a miracle. Within ten minutes he had made it possible for Jeanne to do something that was medically impossible because her foot operations had taken away her ability to bend her toes. They had no joints, only pins holding them.

It convinced Jeanne that she wanted to learn to be a healer and help people the way Elmer had helped her. To her, he was a miracle worker and she idolized him.

She excitedly asked if she could study with him. He agreed but said that she had to move to Orlando where he taught. Jeanne said, "Yes," happily. She knew this was the direction she wanted to go and had been given the opportunity to start with Elmer. She was ready. Her health was good except for a constant pain in her neck.

Besides studying with Elmer, after she moved to Orlando, she was filled with the need to know more about healing and the body. She began reading more esoteric books by Alice Bailey, Annie Besant, Helen Blavatsky and Charles Ledbetter. It was hard to understand their work and Jeanne knew she needed more direction. Astara classes taught the material she had been trying to understand on her own and she signed up for them. One outstanding idea stood out from her classes, that everyone had a subtle body and a colored aura around it that changed colors depending upon the emotional state of the person.

That pesky pain in her neck began bothering Jeanne more and more. Jeanne inquired from friends who might be able to help her and was given the name of Bill Brown, an etheric surgeon. She told Mary Ann about him and asked her to go with her to help her after surgery if she needed it. Elmer was interested in Dr. Bill Brown's work and wanted to go, too. Jeanne paid for his way, not realizing at the time that he was doing mind control on her so she would pay his way.

The three of them were invited to sit in a room filled with people. Dr. Brown was sitting there and went into a trance, a type of meditation that put him in another reality. A Dr. Murphy came into his body and began his diagnosis of Jeanne's problem by asking, "Laddy, laddy you have been in a wreck, if she had been in a wreck. She answered, "No." He became very irritated with her and asked again. She replied, "No," again. Suddenly, Jeanne remembered her mother's car accident when Jeanne was in utero. She asked the spirit if that was the wreck he was thinking of and Spirit agreed. So, Jeanne mentioned her mother's accident and Dr. Murphy left feeling satisfied. Apparently, Jeanne's neck was injured when her mother's car rolled over and over, but not detected when she was a baby.

Another doctor came into Bill's body and began the operation. He took skin, nerve and muscle from Jeanne's bottom and used it to repair her neck. There was no blood loss or the need for anesthetics. The operation took thirty minutes without any of normal procedures that would have been required in a regular hospital.

Although the operation didn't hurt, afterwards, Jeanne had to stay in bed for three days because of the pain that started at the top of her head, went down her body and back up again. There were no two pains at one time. If it hurt in the neck, it didn't hurt in the head or if the pain was in her chest, it wasn't in her neck.

If she had known that she had more pain afterwards than she ever experienced with her foot operations or her hysterectomy she would have prepared by doing some visualization techniques that would have lessened the pain. She asked him before she left why was the recovery so painful if it was a spiritual operation. He replied, "You are new in the field and would never have believed it."

He was right. She never would have believed it. She had thought that by operating on the spiritual level wouldn't hurt in any way, including the recovery. It showed Jeanne that the operation was done on the etheric level which is part of the physical. She had no idea it could feel the same on the etheric as well as on the physical body.

Later in life, she learned that the surgery performed was Piscean. Pisces is the last sign in the zodiac and humanity has just finished the Piscean Age and was not as advanced as we are now.

Jeanne studied with Elmer for one and 1/2 years, but gradually became uneasy around him. She was also confused, upset, and needed guidance about what he was teaching her.

Her next-door neighbor offered to take Jeanne to see a reader who she felt could help Jeanne unravel her concerns about Elmer.

The reader saved Jeanne's life. He told her Elmer was using mind control over her and had been doing so for years. Elmer had done some background checking on Jeanne and learned that her family had money and wanted some of it for himself.

What he told Jeanne made sense to her and she forced herself to accept the fact that Elmer was a charlatan. It didn't make it any easier, however, and she cried bitter tears when she realized her idol had feet of clay. But slowly she became outraged when she thought about what a terrible man he was and what he was doing to so many innocent people who were trying to understand the metaphysical world. Jeanne wanted to expose him and remove his ability to control her mind. It would take five teachers to rid Elmer from her subconscious over a long period of time. As she slowly slipped out of his mind control, she observed his methods more closely.

He charged unsuspecting people anxious to take his classes exorbitant tuitions. At night when they were sleeping, he would travel through the astral to their minds, tell them that the classes were important for them and not expensive. The result was they would not question him the next day. In Jeanne's case, she had written him a huge check, but when she went home and away from his persuasive powers, she was shocked at the amount of money he charged her. She planned on asking for it back the next day. In the meantime, after she was asleep, he would travel through the astral and program her mind into agreeing to accept the huge tuition payment and allow him to keep her check, By the time she awoke the next morning, all her concerns were gone and she was perfectly happy for him to keep her money.

Gradually, she finally confronted Elmer as to why he thought it was alright to do such a terrible thing to her and countless others.

He laughed and said, "I haven't done anything wrong."

"But you have, Elmer. You have used mind control and Black Magic on trusting people.' ﹒"I have grace this lifetime and am pardoned."

"That's your excuse, it's wrong and you know it. You may be a great healer, but you are not a spiritual healer and that's the difference between you and all the great people out there trying to help others. You have used your power to manipulate and control people for your love of money. Remember this Elmer, once we are awakened to something, a truth, or an injustice, we are held accountable to that truth. That is why I wanted to expose you. If you ever acknowledge that you are doing bad things to people through mind control, your life will change dramatically and quickly. And if you ever become aware of the power of forgiveness, instead of greed, your soul will become relentless in reminding you of that truth. Goodbye Elmer. I never want to have anything more to do with you, ever, but I hope you take to heart what I have just told you.

Because of Elmer, she embarked on an entirely different way to learn everything she could about healing. But Elmer had been a good teacher. She had learned an important lesson from him. Unlike Elmer, she would treat everyone she was healing with respect and love.

Be more concerned about your character than your reputation because your character is who you are while your reputation is merely what others think of you. John Wooden

7. STUDYING THE METAPHYSICAL, BECOMING A HEALER, PITFALLS AND ALL

1977-1986

JEANNE

Recovering from Elmer's mind control was a tortuous process. Jeanne moved from Orlando to Spring Hill for four months to study with a teacher named Carlos and a man named Stan and who helped her help rid herself of any remaining vestige of Elmer's mind control over her. Stan and Jeanne spent many a night watching UFOs fly around the town of Brooksville, the county seat adjacent to Springhill. She would watch from her hammock and he from a lounge chair. Neal and David moved to Sarasota and were living together when she was in Spring Hill.

Occasionally, Mary Ann would visit, usually after being in rehab for drugs.

One night, when everyone had settled down for the night, Mary Ann came running into Jeanne's room, screaming,

"Get out of here, get out! That crazy man, Elmer, is in my room shaking my bed. Can't you do something about it?"

Jeanne replied, "We're working on it, Mary Ann. He is really persistent."

"Does he do it very often?"

"It's getting less and less."

"Well, I'm leaving," and she packed up and left that night. She could travel easily because she was no longer was married to Jan and he had custody of their boy, John Marlowe, the third, nicknamed Sonny.

Jeanne felt badly about the way their marriage had dissolved. She blamed Michael for their break-up by encouraging Jan to work away from home for weeks on end, leaving Mary Ann with Carol, Michael's wife who was not at all considerate or hospitable to Mary Ann and her little boy. When Mary Ann asked for a divorce, Jan received custody of Sonny and turned to his sister and brother-in-law to take care of him while he was working. They did it grudgingly.

Elmer continued practicing black magic on Jeanne's group, especially Carlos. A few days later, at a meeting with Carlos and his group, a huge black spider jumped out from nowhere and landed on Carlos. The spider was manifested by Elmer trying to upset Carlos. It was almost pathetic, but Elmer continued to let his presence be known.

It wasn't the first time that Elmer had been in the area physically. He had accompanied Jeanne to a meeting in Brooksville, a year or so before. Before the meeting, he did the unthinkable, he blew Jeanne's chakras open which drained her energy and she became very sick. She had to go lie down and Elmer was delighted. With Jeanne out of the way, he could meet a whole new group of unsuspecting guinea pigs, use his mind control on them and make a lot of money.

It took a long time before Elmer stopped trying to punish

Jeanne and practice black magic, but he finally did. With Carlos and Stan's help, she wiped herself of his influence completely.

Feeling mentally free from Elmer for the first time in months, Jeanne left Spring Hill and moved into a condo on Siesta Key in Sarasota with David and Neal, and occasionally, Mary Ann. Jeanne realized that it was too small to take care of all of them when she saw all of them sleeping in sleeping bags all over the floor. She had to find a bigger home and she did.

.On the first Thanksgiving in Sarasota, Jeanne wanted to have a special dinner to celebrate being there. She began the day preparing the food for their meal and wanted to set the table with her silver and china to make the day even better. When she went to get her silverware from the hall closet, the case was missing. She looked throughout the household items in there, sure that she had put it in there when she moved in. It was gone and Jeanne had her suspicion. Neal had been in the closet one day when she was in the house, and she had seen him. She had a sinking feeling in the pit of her stomach. Neal had sold the silver and the only reason she could think of was for drugs. That meant that her son was a 'druggie!' First, Mary Ann and now Neal was following in her footsteps. As upset as Jeanne was, she comforted herself with the knowledge that addiction ran in Michael's family, and it wasn't surprising that it had happened to her children.

When Jeanne confronted him, Neal wouldn't answer, he just went to bed, complaining of having a stomach ache.

The next thing Neal did was to tell her he had gotten a girl pregnant. Jeanne met the family and the girl's mother looked like she had just come out of the swamp. They wanted Jeanne to marry them because she had become a minister by that time. Everyone came including Michael to the wedding. The service and the fact Jeanne was officiating brought tears to his eyes. It was the first time Jeanne had ever seen him look that way. She knew that he did still have feelings for her, although it was terribly difficult for him to show them.

Neal and his wife stayed together three years before they split up. They had a little girl who Neal and Jeanne took to see his grandmother Nell one time when she was three. Nell did or said something the little girl didn't like, and she said, "F_ck You," to her grandmother and Nell almost fainted. Needless, to say, Nell didn't invite Neal's daughter back to visit her, again.

David was eighteen and dating by then, came home to Jeanne one day and told his mother that he had gotten a girl pregnant. Jeanne couldn't believe that David had done the same thing Neal had a few years before. Jeanne told him she couldn't afford a church wedding, so they were married at Jeanne's home. David pitched in and helped Jeanne clean for the wedding. The bride's father wanted to take pictures and set up several huge spotlights that were very hot after a little while. The father took pictures of Michael and the family using the lights. Michael was full of alcohol, and he began to sweat. It came pouring out of him and soaked his shirt. He asked Jeanne for another one which she provided and said, "Tell that guy to turn off those lights, if he wants me in his pictures."

David and his wife, Mary Ann, had a baby girl named Alisha. They stayed together for several years and then divorced. His wife moved to New York and married a Columbian. For years David fought to see his daughter and finally was able to see her on a regular basis.

Through acquaintances, Jeanne met Sally Vickers, a trans- medium and immediately liked her. When Sally offered Jeanne, a job transcribing her sessions and putting them on tape, Jeanne accepted without hesitation. It was a great learning experience for Jeanne, and it paid the bills. She worked for Sally for three years and learned a great deal from Sally.

Sally made continual predictions about the future which fascinated Jeanne. She made personal predictions to Jeanne and many of her clients. She also made world-wide predictions; the end of the USSR and the fall of the Berlin Wall, before President

Reagan made his famous plea to the world, the explosion on the NASA space shuttle, and finally, the enormous changes in the world's weather patterns.

During those three years, the name of a Mr. Gibson came up, occasionally as a healer who had developed an interesting way to heal. The more Jeanne heard about the method, the more she wanted to talk to him and learn more about it. She decided to talk to him in person. It meant going to St. Petersburg, VA where he lived. She understood that his church, called the Temple of the Living God was where he kept his appointments. The technique she was interested in was called aura balancing. She would have him balance her auras to experience the technique. Asking for an appointment to see him, she was told he was booked and leaving right after he finished his last appointment. Disappointed, but not dissuaded, she had a premonition that they would meet, soon.

Turning her attention to another wish she had, having her soul portrait done, she contacted a well-known person in healing circles, named Violet who did soul portraits, which is what the reader sees as the spirit of the person. Jeanne made an appointment with her for the following weekend. It meant she would need to drive to Tarpon Springs, Florida, but because it was something she had always wanted, she was happy to make the trip from Sarasota.

When she met Violet, Jeanne felt very comfortable with her. Their time together was very satisfying, and the soul portrait Violet did for Jeanne was beautiful.

Afterwards, when they were finished and having tea, Violet said, "I have a visitor who you might like to meet. His name is Ron Gibson."

"He's here! Small world, Violet, I tried to see him last weekend and he was too busy. I'm delighted to get another chance."

"Of course," Violet said as if she knew Ron's being

there was no accident.

After introductions, Jeanne asked him if he would do an aura balancing on her. He stared at her and finally said, "I will have to ask Spirit."

Jeanne thought, I don 't like his attitude. Using Spirit as an excuse as to whether he'll work on me is ridiculous. It's rude and inconsiderate.

But he did come back and say, "Yes, you will be a good subject."

She felt a little foolish for being so quick to judge after being accepted so enthusiastically.

When she got off his table, she had many feelings. She had a feeling of well-being, slightly spacy, but connected to a gentle light. It so moved her, she told Ron, elatedly, "That's what I want the rest of my life.'

Ron smiled at her and said, "It was very successful, and your auras balanced nicely."

"Thanks, would you like to give a workshop in Sarasota about this process? I will be glad to sponsor you!"

Ron thought for a moment or two and then said, "Yes, I think it would be a great opportunity."

As she drove home, she reflected on the healing and thought, everything about it felt right. I know I want to heal people using this approach. Thank you, Spirit, for leading in my quest to find my way.

She couldn't wait to tell Sally what she had done and who was coming to give a workshop. Sally was very pleased to learn about Ron Gibson and his up-coming workshop.

When Ron arrived, being very charismatic, he made friends easily with Sally. His workshop was a success and Jeanne was reassured that this was what she wanted to do after seeing how well people accepted his workshop.

When Jeanne met Henry at Ron's workshop, she felt an

immediate attraction to him, quickly forgetting the promise she made to herself not to date again. She also noticed that Ron, who was openly gay, was very attentive to Henry, too.

During the workshop, when she talked with Henry, they became good friends. Henry asked Jeanne to take care of him after he had an operation which she agreed to, but it was a disaster for Jeanne because he spent the whole-time recuperating, calling, and talking to an old girlfriend.

When he recovered, they began to date more and more, and Jeanne spent time at his place where he had a nursery business. Jeanne learned the nursery business from him on her visits to his place. One day, she and he had just come out of one of the nursery buildings where they had been putting lady bugs on the plants to eat the aphids and Henry wanted to take a swim in his above ground pool. Jeanne spent the time while he was swimming watching an angel in the sky. It was enormous and looked like a painting as it stayed there motionless for a long time.

They had a lot of spiritual experiences going to churches and doing meditations. Henry began helping Jeanne with her healings until his sexual energies became too much for Jeanne. He would project his sexuality as he was working, and Jeanne had to stop his participation.

After a massage class that he and Jeanne had taken, they went out to the beach and were lying in the sun. Henry was next to another woman who had also taken the class and began flirting with her. Henry was a big flirt.

Jeanne decided to break up with him after two years because of his continual flirting with other women. She was tired of him and his antics. She moved to a group of condos called the Meadows at the edge of town. Her children were all gone, and she was alone. She sponsored speakers on a regular basis. She also continued working with her pendants doing aura balancing on her clients. She bought her stones and pendants from Bill Williams rock shop. He and his wife would sit with Jeanne for hours talking about stones and what healing properties they had.

He also showed her how strong the energy of the stones were by putting a picture of an ill person in with the stones as they were being tumbled and polished and how much better the person would feel afterwards.

With each client she used the stones that she felt appropriate and twirled each one in a circular motion over the body of her client. As each stone's energy moved down into the cellular level of the individual, it lifted out the negative energy patterns and removed them. When her clients had much the same reaction as she had had with Ron, Jeanne knew she was on the right healing path.

Bill Williams gave her a bag of rose quartz stones which she placed in her apartment's glassed in porch.

She also went to Venice, Florida to study the 'Keys of Enoch,' taken from the bible. While there she was introduced to Billie a woman who used a light potential meter which could read the subconscious mind. It was an awesome machine and Jeanne was invited to sit with Billie and watch her work with clients. The machine would register the release of the negative emotions.

While she was there, she went to a reader who drew auras and in Jeanne's aura drawing she drew a picture of a man who had a black mustache. Jeanne didn't like him being in her drawing, but it was there for a reason.

When she returned to Sarasota, during her healing sessions with her clients, after the actual healing with the stones, Jeanne spent time helping them to use a visualization technique that she had slowly developed to help her recover from a nervous breakdown years before.

To begin with, she explained the power of both positive and negative emotions, emphasizing that negative emotions always drained people and made them sick. Jeanne had a white board which she put in front of the client and with the client's eyes closed ask the person to visualize all his/her negative feelings such as hate, rage, guilt, shame, humiliation, and revenge, betrayal, mistrust, grief, denial, and lack of self-love, put it on the board and then erase it with divine love. She then asked the person to see the board white which means that the subconscious sees it gone and will release the emotional memories. That was the essence of what Jeanne was trying to do. She always ended the session with a healing prayer, asking them to participate in the following:

I claim my Divine right to choose what I will hold in my consciousness and my energy field.

Through the power of my indwelling Christ, I decree that all my past vows of poverty, celibacy and obedience taken anytime, anyplace, under any circumstances during any incarnation be at this moment released from my consciousness. I release all emotions surrounding the vow back to the Light. I bless this energy as I return it to the source. I forgive all pain and people around the circumstances of the vow.

Whatever limits and misperceptions that have held the vow in place are now dissolved. Into the vacuum now pour clarity, creativity, and abundance. I freely choose to accept the grace of the indwelling Christ.

Thank You Mother-Father God

When appropriate, Jeanne explained another healing technique that came from the Hawaiian Islands called pulling AKA cords.

[Note: Ho'oponopono -Hawaiian Code of Forgiveness teaches that when you meet another person you establish a connection with them (called and aka cord)] that develop between individuals or groups who work together or otherwise meet.]

The cord always attaches to the weakest part of the body. For example, if someone does not say what needs to be said, his or her throat chakra shuts down because the cords are blocking it. Mentally, one must visualize pulling out cords and burn them so the throat chakra can re-open. Then visualize the ashes becoming light. One never cuts the cords because part of them will be left in the person to cause future trouble. All of them must be pulled out and burned.

Positive and negative cords can also be connected to inanimate objects like houses, hospitals, cars, tractors, golf clubs, anything holding an emotional meaning to an individual.

In the circles that Jeanne traveled in, several people had mentioned a bookstore to her in Sarasota that catered to metaphysical interests. Books, stones, crystals, cards, incense, healing oils and some jewelries were sold there. It intrigued Jeanne and she wanted to see what they offered for herself.

A woman named Jane owned it but was basically run by a dark-haired man named Chris and a young woman friend of his. When Jeanne walked into the store for the first time and saw him, she was stunned. He was the same man as the one in her aura portrait.

At first Jeanne was taken in by the guy. They were going to work together, but after a while, she saw what was happening and backed off after he tried to do some Black Magic on her two or three different occasions.

Jeanne traveled in a circle of some spiritual friends and some not so friendly. One evening she was invited to her friends' home for dinner. As Jeanne walked in, she recognized a woman there whom Jeanne knew practiced Black Magic. The hosts had invited the woman even though Jeanne had advised the couple about her, but they had ignored Jeanne's warning.

Sensing she was in danger from the woman, Jeanne tried to avoid her, but sometime during the evening, the woman had sent a mental psychic attack on Jeanne causing her such pain that she fell to the floor.

As Jeanne became more acquainted with that group of people, she decided they were all capable of practicing Black Magic and stopped seeing them. Later, she heard that Jane, the owner of the bookstore had tried to kill a woman with Black Magic because she wanted the woman's husband. She tried to get rid of her by planting seeds of fear in her head about the health of her body. The woman ended up having a breast removed fearing cancer which wasn't there and having her gall bladder out unnecessarily.

Jeanne's clients began dwindling down after a year or so and began sponsoring speakers to come and lecture on new and different spiritual material to help them and help her business. She learned, unhappily, that some of the men that she sponsored had feet of clay and were much too interested sexually with some of the clients that came to the workshops and afterwards for healings. She stopped the workshops because she didn't trust the men and decided to travel to all of the healing centers, she knew in the South to find sponsors for her workshops on her aura balancing technique. Her workshops usually produced clients and some financial reward.

After covering many miles and several states, she was very upset with the spiritual centers she had contacted. No one would sponsor her and let her give a workshop. One night, after a very disappointing day, she ended up in Durham, North Carolina. She went to a liquor store, bought a bottle of wine, went to her room, sat in the middle of her bed, and began cussing and drinking.

She yelled to the empty room, "I am going to quit this line of work because I haven't been able to find one person willing to give me a job or sponsor me! Do you hear me, Spirit? I'm through unless you help me." She finished the bottle of wine and went to bed. The next morning, she got in her car and said, "I'm damn well going home," but something told her to drive to Black Mountain, North Carolina, instead and meet with Jim Blake, the head of the center.

Not sure why she was going there, when she arrived, she got out of the car, went into the office, and asked, "Is Jim Blake here?"

"No, he's out, but we expect him soon."

Again, filled with disappointment, she said, "Tell him I'm going to spend some time in the special room with the lights."

When he returned, and learned Jeanne was there, he went looking for her and asked her to join him in his office and catch-up on her life. She did and explained that she hadn't been very well received anywhere."

Jim started laughing and said, "I'll fix that, Tuesday night you will do a lecture on aura balancing and Wednesday you will start working for me using your healing technique on everyone who is interested."

Amazed and delighted that he had been so wonderful to her, she said, gratefully,

"Thanks, Jim, I can't wait to get started."

After the workshop, thirty people signed up for a healing receiving an aura balancing. Jeanne couldn't believe her good fortune but was concerned about how she would see all those people in three days.

Each day she felt more fatigued but was determined to help as many people as signed up for their healing. She made friends with Gary, an Apache Indian. He fascinated her with his stories of Indian lore. She also met Robyn, an admirer who brought her lunch every day and talked with her about her work. They became fast friends, although Jim Blake warned her about him, saying that he was crazy and to watch out for him.

The last day she was there, Jim invited her to stay at his home. She was very tired and wanted to just get through her healings, but he was very insistent. She felt obligated to some degree to accept his hospitality and so she agreed, against her better judgment. She had heard, via the grapevine that any good looking, interesting female would be subject to Jim's advances if they stayed at his home, overnight.

Sure enough, at three o'clock in the morning, Jim appeared in her room in the astral, hoping to have a sexual encounter with her, but Jeanne was ready for him and said, "No, Jim, this wasn't part of the deal."

The next day, he was very distant towards her, and she knew he was mad at her and her rebuff, but gradually became more amiable. He asked Jeanne if she would give his wife and daughter healings. Thinking, I'm ready to drop, she agreed. After working with them, Jim asked her to give him a healing. She thought, he really believes in my work which is a great honor and I owe it to him for all he had done for me. She said she would be glad to do it, although it took every ounce of her strength to do it.

Jeanne left, financially well paid, but physically and mentally exhausted. Reaching home, she gratefully went to bed and spent most of the next three weeks recovering. Spirit had heard her request to heal and answered her with three days of non-stop work!

While she was recovering, Jeanne heard from an old friend, Rosemary Watson who was very involved with the Aquarian Research Center in West Palm Beach. She asked Jeanne if she would be interested in working for her at the center. Jeanne agreed immediately. She had always gotten along with Rosemary, and she was wonderful about keeping Jeanne booked with clients. She worked there every six weeks giving many lectures on aura balancing and healing her clients. It was there that she added the Sacred Flame Ritual.

She began the healing with Om chanting. When everyone was relaxed and quiet, she would ask them to focus on the flame on the altar in front of the Eucharist and feel its presence. After sufficient time, Jeanne would ask them to let their body settle into the flame.

She would then repeat the chant of Om with them joining in and ask them to visualize:

Jesus stepping off the cross, triumphant. Repeating the chant, she would strike a match to light her candle and say:

"The sacred flame is visible

May all hearts be open and reminded

Light is my very nature

When the universe manifests itself

Verily, then it is I
that shines I am
the Light of the
world

I am not other than Light."

Initiation — Source of flame is singular

Intent - To go within, have each person light their candle from yours.

Repeat Om chant together, after leader

Put out candle — internalizing the flame — mingling the sacred fire that you are bringing inside of them

Together chant — three times - Clients relight their candle and recite chant once. Leader blows out their flame, bringing it within.

Become one with intent

Candle placed on altar to continue burning, extinguished when everyone left.

Jeanne worked there for three years, learned a lot, but felt it was time to move on to learn more. She moved to Asheville, North Carolina where her longtime friend, Jim Blake was the head of the Light Center at Black Mountain. She had known him for a long time; sponsored him in Florida at the center in West Palm beach, had known him in Brooksville when she was living in Spring Hill and always felt spiritually connected to him.

Jeanne made house calls occasionally and was out on one on a snowy winter's day across the river from the center. Just a few flakes had been falling when she crossed the bridge to make her house call, but when she finished her healing and started back home, there was a big storm. The driving was bad on the roads and the bridge was a sheet of ice that she had to re-cross to get home. When she pulled up and saw what was facing her, she asked Spirit to melt the ice so she could drive across safely. She continued her prayer for about fifteen minutes. Slowly, the ice melted off the bridge road and Jeanne was able to drive over it successfully. When she walked in, she thanked Spirit for always taking care of her.

Although she liked Jim, had many clients at the Light Center, and was financially comfortable, she was getting restless. She hadn't wasted her spare time. She studied and became an ordained minister of Alliance of Divine Love. The ministry's home was based in Florida but had spread to Asheville. At first, she worked as a minister and gave sermons every week, which got old quickly for Jeanne. She didn't want that type of work. She was a healer. She made her excuses and quit.

She had also taken the opportunity to rid herself of her terrible, confused feelings about the Civil War. The war had preyed upon her mind for a long time, and she began spending long hours watching the series, North and South. Although the movie didn't show the raping's, castrations, and hangings, just the intimations made her throw-up. Coming from somewhere inside of her were powerful emotions that she couldn't understand. She forced herself to watch the series until she no longer became nauseous. She felt better about what she had done but knew there was more to it.

During the time Jeanne worked at the center, she met

Dudley Bird, who became a good friend. Dudley introduced Jeanne to a reader who gave her a reading that she will never forget. The woman described Jeanne as standing on the top of mountain in a white chiffon dress. Jeanne was holding up her arms and pleading, "Please God give me the strength to get through this lifetime." The reading immediately lifted Jeanne's spirits.

In her twenties, Jeanne had seen the movie, "Leave Her to Heaven", where the actress stood at the top of the stairs in a white dress asking for help. That scene gave Jeanne goosebumps, and she didn't know why. Now she did.

Go confidently in the direction of your dreams. Live the life you have imagined.   Henry David Thoreau.

8. MOVNG NORTH
ON HER SEARCH

1986-1994

Jeanne

Her friend, Dudley, who lived in Madison, Virginia called one day and asked if Jeanne would like to come up to Virginia in Gordonsville and house-sit. Dudley said that Jeanne would like the change and love the owner. Dudley was a good salesperson and Jeanne agreed. She was ready for a new opportunity to use her talents.

Jeanne was not surprised when she met Tommie, the owner. Dudley was a good judge of character. Tommie was a warm and friendly woman who loved her home but was going to travel and wanted someone to take care of her place. She showed Jeanne around the home. As she followed Tommie through the five-bedroom, five-bathroom plantation house, she learned that the home and grounds had been there before, during and after the Civil War to the present day. She confided in Jeanne that it had a resident ghost or two living there. One was a young southern lady about eighteen who wore a wide-brimmed hat and long dress and the other one hid out in a suit of armor next to the front door.

"Do you mind ghosts? Mine are very nice and nothing to be afraid of, but the one in the suit of armor is quite a tease."

"What does he do?"

"He loves to turn the lights on and off just when I'm having company. And if I leave the dining room light on as a night light down here before I go to bed, he turns it off."

After Tommie left and she moved in, Jeanne could see eyes looking out at her from inside the mask. She wasn't disturbed by the young woman, but the ghost in the armor did like to tease. He did turn the lights on and off at will.

Jeanne asked, "Please leave the dining room light on so I can see if I have to come downstairs to investigate something in the middle of the night."

"When the owner comes home, you can do as you please, you can play games with Tommie, but not when I'm here alone."

The ghost honored Jeanne's request and always left it on, but the day Tommie was expected back, the ghost turned off the dining room lights. He was a fun ghost to live with, Jeanne chuckled at its antics and distinctly heard someone laugh in return.

Throughout her stay, Jeanne loved walking down the sweeping staircase reminiscent of Scarlett O'Hara's home. But outside beyond the fence around the house, Jeanne was always hit with an ominous energy which nauseated her the closer she came to the tower on the property. On her walk around the property with Tommie before she left, Jeanne had learned that during the days of slavery, the overseer of the plantation spent a great deal of time in the tower. She had had a similar attack of nausea when she visited a Virginia estate which her son, Neal managed. There it happened when she walked past a big barn on the estate. The feeling dissipated, however, when she reached the beautiful pond that Neal had cleaned and filled with water plants. Wild ducks liked it too.

While Neal was working on the estate, he met Roberta and started dating her. Roberta was very knowledgeable about the history of the area because she taught history of the south at

Sweetbriar College. Neal introduced Jeanne to her, and Roberta told Jeanne all about the history of the area including Tommie's home and grounds.

Through friends, Jeanne learned of a lady in Warrenton Virginia, Michaelle Jones who had the spiritual ability to clear the areas of wandering soldiers' souls and send them on their way to the light of the Universe and find peace. She was thorough. She even cleared the trees and bushes of the dense energy lurking near the battle fields or on the plantations that brutalized slaves.

Dudley and Jeanne knew they needed her help to teach them how to learn to rid their properties of the agony caused by war and slavery. It was an involved process requiring their belief that it was possible. After hours of walking the land, meditating, and praying they were successful, Jeanne was no longer nauseated when she went to Tommie's barn.

At the same time, Jeanne knew she should become part of the community by attending courses and services at the local Unity Church but was busy with settling into her rental. When Anne, Jeanne's friend, who was teaching a course in metaphysics at the time at the local Unity Church, said, "Jeanne, I need your expertise. Would you teach Reiki in two weeks? You would be great."

Jeanne agreed hesitantly because she knew as a Virgo, she had to plan and organize before she could do it. She knew she'd have to do a lot of work to gather her thoughts and her material and prepare for her assignment. She was glad that Anne had encouraged her to teach again. In two weeks, she was ready and taught a thorough course in Reiki explaining the three levels and what is involved in becoming a Reiki Master, the highest form of Reiki.

When Tommie returned, Jeanne moved into Charlottesville. She shared a duplex with her friend, Anne, and began acclimating herself into the healing community.

However, Anne had to leave soon after to live in Arizona hoping the Arizona climate would help clear her body of bronchitis.

As Jeanne reacquainted herself with the community and friends, the name John Perry kept coming to her in different ways; through fliers sent to her by friends, or she would meet someone who would mention his name as a healer and sing his praises. After hearing about him and having received three fliers, she knew she was being directed to meet him. She picked up the phone, called him and after introducing herself and talking with him for a little while, she liked what he had to offer. She said she would like to sponsor him if he was interested in talking to a group of seekers in Charlottesville. He accepted her offer and said his workshop would cover numerology and the Coptic belief system. Jeanne was personally interested in both of his areas of expertise and told him she would enjoy his workshop, too.

They set a convenient date for both. The night he was to come in February, it was snowing. Jeanne was concerned that his plane would be grounded, and he wouldn't be able to make it. She had a house full of people coming to hear him.

But he came. When he got off the plane, he recognized her immediately because she told him she would be wearing her mink coat, a long-ago gift from Michael. But there was more. They both felt a definite connection to each other. Perhaps, they had been together in past lives and their souls recognized each other.

As they discussed their feelings for each other on the way to her home, John made an incredible statement. He said with authority that he knew they had come to Earth ages ago, from another universe to help Earth develop faster into a lighter, less dense planet. He had fathered a human baby with her but apologized for leaving her and returning to a different planet. A reader told her later that in this lifetime she was spiritually, but not physically connected to John, which was not a surprise to Jeanne.

The next evening when the people came to hear him speak, he took on a different persona and acted like he was a god. He ordered Jeanne around in front of her guests until she questioned her offer to sponsor him. However, he gave a good workshop, and all was forgiven including his chauvinistic attitude.

While he was staying with her, she did a healing for him using her aura balancing technique. He was so impressed with the way it made him feel that he invited her to come to his next conference in Michigan at Olivet College outside of Grand Rapids and teach her technique to the students.

She was pleased to be offered a chance to explain aura balancing and give healings using it. At the conference, John was a true friend, promoted her work, praised her ability to heal and attracted a lot of interested people to sign up for her classes. She taught classes in aura balancing and the Coptic ministry. John introduced her to many people. As a result, she was offered jobs on the spiritual circuit. In return, she was so appreciative to John that she gave the Coptic Organization gifts of money and free classes. And later after a trip to England, she gave him a replica of Excalibur and a beautiful emerald.

Being on the circuit meant Jeanne would financially make a living doing what she loved, lecturing, and giving healing workshops on aura balancing and patterns of behavior all over the country. After five years of traveling, however, she made the decision to stop. She was burned out.

During her travels, she had met many new friends. One couple, in particular, Janet and Warren, who had sponsored her became close friends. They had a son who they loved very deeply that lived in Hawaii and was dying, but because of terrible financial problems had given up the idea of seeing him. Jeanne financed their trip because she was financially solvent. In gratitude, Warren built Jeanne a massage table that was gorgeous and became her healing table.

To finance his conferences, John and his wife owned a travel business and set-up tours, with interested clients to places he felt would have spiritual meaning for them. His fee covered his expenses and made money for their business. It was a good arrangement for all. Jeanne always made time for his trips.

In the early 1990s, Jeanne traveled with him in a group to England. John was fascinated and quite knowledgeable about the mystical world of King Arthur and the Knights of the Round Table. They were on a bus going to King Arthur's castle and Jeanne looked out of the bus window and saw the sign: King Arthur's Motel. Jeanne announced, "We are going to stop here and stay" and John said, "No."

Jeanne repeated, "Yes, we are," and directed the driver to drive in. He did and everyone was delighted to get off the bus. When Jeanne walked in, she looked to her right and there was a magnificent replica of the Round Table with the names of the knights on it. The motel was set on a big bluff overlooking the water and the owners claimed that Merlin's cave was down at the water's edge. So, everyone climbed down the side of the hill to see what they could find. Jeanne took a picture of the cave and when it was developed it had captured a male figure in the picture that they had not seen with the naked eye.

On the trip to Egypt, he asked Jeanne to accompany he and his wife. During the trip, the tour traveled to Karnak. There, the guides spoke of an ancient tunnel that started in the Yucatan and went under the Atlantic Ocean to Egypt. They also spoke of a lake resembling the shape of the United States that is an entrance, too, for the UFOs. The interest in the lake made the government fence it off from onlookers. But that doesn't stop UFOs.

During the trip, John spoke highly of Jeanne's abilities as a healer to the members of the group and because of his praise, a woman approached Jeanne for a healing. The gossip afterwards was that a woman named Linda Rankins, a member of the staff and apparently jealous of Jeanne's ability went to the client and insinuated that Jeanne's work was not what it should be. Jeanne began to watch Linda's subtle manipulations to play down Jeanne's ability and promote herself to John.

John also arranged a trip to Corsica to see the castle where Robin Hood had supposedly lived. From there they went to France to Rennes Le Chateau, a church built by the Templars where it was rumored held buried treasure of that whole area. There was an imposing sculpture of Pan, the earth god, at the beginning of the large main hall. Across the room, was a painting of John the Baptist baptizing Jesus Christ. Next to the painting were two metaphysically colored black and white chess games symbolizing the game of life.

On the next level, there was a font made in the shape of a clam shell. The clam shell is symbolic of Venus or Aphrodite who was born of a clam shell and the holy font of the Catholics.

Upstairs to another level, there was a sculpture of a salamander who is symbolic of a fire spirit. Also, on that level, there were four angels making the symbol of the equal arm cross, which represented the four directions, north, south, east, and west and the four elements, air, water, fire and metal. It was also the type of cross the Templar Knights used. In front of the apex in a pyramid there was a big cross that represented the crucifixion of life. In the apex, the Sermon on the Mount was displayed.

That display was particularly important to Jeanne who had spent years studying the various interpretations of the sermon and concluded that the accepted version was wrong. She felt that the true meaning of the sermon had been altered and the real blueprint for living that Christ had intended was not being told. If interpreted correctly, it was the true way human beings should live their lives.

Each stained-glass window in the church contained a spiritual figure. One of them showed Jesus and his twin brother. All of them were lit electrically except for Hermes, the god of thought. Every year on January 17th, the sun was in a perfect position to shine directly on Hermes, lighting him up. Hermes' book in his lap was closed. His accepted message was "open the book of your life, do not keep it closed, go learn of all the wonders that are out there just waiting for you to discover."

The inn where the group was staying had a large chair carved out of stone displayed prominently out in front of the building. It was dubbed by the local people as the devil's chair because of the many healing myths surrounding it when people sat in it.

One of the women on the tour had great difficulty climbing-up any stairs or walking-up any incline without losing her breath. To catch her breath after any walk, she automatically sat down in the huge chair before she went into the inn. One day, a miracle occurred when she did that. She immediately felt better and for the rest of the trip was able to walk everywhere with no problem. When Jeanne saw how the woman responded to the chair, she sat in it and felt an immediate influx of energy enveloping her.

While the rooms were sufficient for the normal needs of the guests, the building also had a beautiful meditation room that was open to the guests. Early one morning, not being able to sleep, Jeanne had a tremendous urge to visit the meditation room. She had hardly settled into her meditation when a group of druids came in from Stonehenge, England and sat down. Seeing her alone, they invited her to join them in their meditation.

She was delighted and moved into their circle. They began chanting their mantra, the vowel sounds, A E I O U, drawn out slowly in a low humming sound. Jeanne felt a closeness to them that was indefinable as she became one with them in their mantra and meditation. She knew she was supposed to have been there with them that morning. It was another mystical experience for Jeanne and something that she would never forget.

On the plane ride home, Jeanne was surprised to find herself sitting next to Linda. Linda had evidently exchanged seats with the person that had been Jeanne's flying companion. During the whole flight, Linda barraged Jeanne with questions about John and Nancy. Were they happily married? Where was each of them from? What kind of families did they come from? Were the families well off? Where did they meet? Linda went on and on questioning Jeanne during the whole trip about John and Nancy's background and history.

Linda's aggressive attitude made Jeanne feel very uncomfortable. She tried to deflect Linda's questions, but Linda would circle around coming back to the same questions all during the trip. Jeanne wondered what were Linda's motives? Why was she so determined to dig into John and Nancy's lives? At an opportune moment, Jeanne went to John with her concerns. She was shocked by his response. He simply told her she was jealous and brushed her off. Jeanne became more and more suspicious of Linda and her motives.

Every year, John returned to Mount Shasta, California, the home of the UFOs. He and his wife, Nancy, Jeanne, and Linda took a group of interested people to visit the mountain, too. It drew all kinds of spiritual seekers drawn to meditation on the mountain. On one occasion, their group came upon a group of nude hikers who asked them to join them in meditation. John's expression was priceless as he stood with his group, meditating with the nudists. Some of the nudists became aroused, which became obvious to Jeanne's party. She knew it was just a matter of time before John took his group to another part of the mountain.

Although Jeanne hadn't told John, her real reason for her

trip was to get in touch with the 'I Am,' people who lived near Mt. Shasta. She had become very interested in their view of God and life and had read all their books on the subject. She had read about their special meditation chapel that held the 'Great Flame,' a special light that enhanced the whole meditating experience. Jeanne wanted to see the chapel and sought out one of the overseers to ask to see it. They became friends in the process and had long conversations about the 'I Am' belief system.

The group's guide was a young woman who was studying to go into a Zen monastery. Jeanne also became friends and she offered to take Jeanne to visit the Zen monastery. When the rest of the group found out about it, they wanted to go too, and so everyone went and meditated in the Zen monastery.

The plan was to try and see UFOs. It was a common belief among people who studied UFOs, that they went underground into Mt. Shasta to an existing world inside the earth. It was the reason UFOs came down there. One afternoon, when she and John were sitting on the side of Mount Shasta a UFO came down parallel with Jeanne, and hovered next to her. She had evidently gone into another dimension to be aware of them because they were invisible to people who weren't on their wavelength.

She asked John, "Do you see the UFO next to me?" He didn't. Jeanne was excited. It was one of the most eerie, delightful sights to experience that she had had for some time.

During their trip home, again, Linda incessantly asked Jeanne all kinds of questions pertaining to Jeanne's work. When Jeanne tried to talk to John about how strange Linda's interest in her work was, he brushed her off again and said she was just jealous of Linda.

Jeanne was certain there was more to the whole situation than John was willing to admit. She knew instinctively that she was not inside the loop any more with John and wondered if he was interested in Linda personally. As time went on, Linda gradually worked her way further into John's organization, becoming very indispensable to him. John setting up the conference schedule, pitted Linda against Jeanne having Linda teach the same courses at the workshop. Linda began teaching a course in patterns and the Coptic course in ministry which had been exclusively Jeanne's courses. Jeanne was furious when she found out what he had done. In essence they were taken away from her and it hurt terribly. The other blow that befell her was the Coptic Board's decision not to help her keep her ministerial license current. It only cost the organization twenty-five dollars a month, but they wouldn't pay it for her.

After she had given so much to their group,
she felt betrayed. It was time to quit.

While Jeanne was still living in Charlottesville and traveling to the Coptic Center in Michigan, for conferences, an old friend, Peggy Fitzgerald contacted both Jeanne and John explaining that she would like to talk with them about teaching a leadership course. The three of them met and developed a course for John and Jeanne to teach in Abington, Virginia. It would be offered three times a year to interested people, including Peggy. From that beginning, Peggy started a conference in Johnson City, Tennessee each year and it continued, for over twenty-five years.

Because Jeanne and Peggy's personalities complimented each other, Peggy asked Jeanne to work with her on her conference each year after that.

Back in Charlottesville, Jeanne had been forced to move to a smaller apartment because her friend, Anne, had moved to Arizona for her health. Although Jeanne worked at Virginia Dominion Power for several years, it was still hard to make ends meet. But working there meant she had another group of people who were interested in the basic rudiments of spirituality. She taught them about crystals, auras, and their souls. For Christmas, she gave everyone in her office a crystal. The vice president used to stand by her desk and listen while she answered questions about metaphysics. On the weekends, Jeanne continued her aura balancing on people who wanted to be healed.

One day she came home from work and her front door was open. When Jeanne saw that, she called her mother and her mother said, "Go find a house and I'll buy it for you."

Jeanne contacted her friend Dudley who was a real estate agent. They had fun renewing their friendship and looking at places to buy. Jeanne's credit rating was bad because she had been forced to declare bankruptcy, but her mother's pockets were deep. Knowing this, Jeanne decided on a place in Gordonsville that had a pond which attracted crickets. The noise they made when Jeanne was looking over the property was unbelievable. Jeanne decided they were welcoming her.

"I'm supposed to buy this place," she told Dudley. She was further drawn to it because of its beauty and history. It had been built in 1840 and was used as a hospital during the Civil War. She bought it in 1986 when it was one hundred and forty-six years old. Why buy such an old place?

She soon learned that her home was inhabited by many unwanted entities, and she needed help. When Dudley explained her new technique to help Jeanne, she welcomed Dudley with open arms. Every week, Dudley would come and visualize a big net under Jeanne's house and property. Slowly she would lift it until it was above the roof and tree line. Once cleared, she visualized tying the net together tightly and sending it out into the Universe toward the light.

Dudley was successful in clearing out most of the nasty entities and left the more gentle, benign ones alone. Jeanne's cat had fun all night every night, chasing them off Jeanne's bed.

During the time on her farm, she invited Gary, an Apache friend of hers she had met in Asheville to visit her at her farm. He built sweat lodges and medicine wheels on the property and gave workshops. It was time for great learning for Jeanne about

Indian spiritualism. They used her house and property well. Many people came for healing and Jeanne felt it was a great investment being able to help so many people. Jeanne loved living there. But the cost of up-keep was unbelievable. Jeanne tried to help herself financially by teaching a leadership course at Shenandoah Crossing, but it wasn't enough. When she sold it, she knew the good memories she had of her time there would stay with her, always. She owned the house for eight years from 1986-1994.

Never believe that a few caring people can't change the world. For indeed, that's all who ever have.

Margaret Mead

9. ON THE MOVE, AGAIN, LOOKING OR ANSWERS

1995-2000

Jeanne

In 1994 Jeanne sold her home, happy to get out from under all the expensive up-keep and move to Hilton Head, North Carolina. She had been invited to help her friend, Diane, who was very ill. They had been friends for a long time starting when they were high school chums at The Cathedral. She and Diane had revived their friendship during a reunion at school that year and that was when Diane had suggested that Jeanne move to Hilton Head. Jeanne jumped at the chance.

Jeanne loved Diane's parents, who also lived there part of the year and couldn't wait to see them again. Jeanne worked with Diane during the time she was alive to help her let go of the past and forgive herself. Diane died four months later, and Jeanne knew why she had gone to Hilton head, to give Diane peace.

Jeanne was living in Hilton Head when she got word that her mother was very ill. Jeanne was taking care of Mary Ann's son Justin while his mother was on a ski trip. Jeanne packed up Justin and they drove to Tampa/St. Petersburg where her mother was in the hospital. Jeanne and Justin stayed at Mary Ann's apartment and Jeanne spent time in the hospital with her mother. Jeanne felt sorry for her mother, but any love she might have had for her had disappeared long ago. The funeral was a social funeral, and the minister gave the eulogy. Her sister, Nell Leigh received the lion's share of her mother's estate, over a Million dollars. Jeanne received Eighty-Five Thousand dollars and some property at Lake Homosassa.

After Diane died, Jeanne attended a conference in Michigan at Olivet College and met Rob Ranger. He offered her the chance to take courses at his hypnosis school. Jeanne liked the idea, went back to Hilton Head, contacted Rob, he found her a place to live, and she left for Lansing, Michigan. She began by working in the administration, setting up the materials for his school, selling books and doing clerical Work in exchange for taking hypnosis courses. The following year she obtained a teaching position from Rob. She also taught courses, once a year at Olivet College for John's conference in Grand Rapids. She was quickly becoming a good teacher through practice.

During those years of teaching, Jeanne met Sheryl, a fellow teacher. Their personalities clicked and Sheryl became one of Jeanne's best friends. Her husband, Frank, was a hypnotherapist and well known in his field. Sheryl encouraged her husband to apply for a teaching job in the school, too, which he did, but jealous Rob never allowed it.

Jeanne met many people as a teacher and one woman named Belinda took a liking to Jeanne. She wanted Jeanne to go to Hawaii with her and help sponsor an acquaintance of hers and help with the conference. Jeanne liked the idea of going to Hawaii again but told Belinda that she didn't have the money to go. Belinda assured her if she would help with the conference, she would pay all her expenses.

Belinda proved very difficult to work with and was rumored to being a lesbian. Jeanne wished she hadn't said yes so quickly. The trip turned out to be an awful one. While she was there, she had a car wreck, something she had never experienced in all her years of driving. Paying for the damages ate into the small amount of money Jeanne ended up making. Belinda was very picky, and Jeanne counted the days until she could leave and return to Lansing. She did one thing that she wanted to do before she left, visit many of the churches on the island. While on her tour she would always remember the weather pattern in the sky. It turned dark in the middle of the day and something about that bothered Jeanne. When she returned to the hotel, she had a call from her son, Neal. He said in a choking voice, "Mary Ann is dying. Mom, please come home and see her before she dies.

We must let go of the life we have planned, so we can have the life that is waiting for us.

Joseph Campbell

10. SHARING HER GIFTS

2000-2007

JEANNE

On August 5th of 2000, Mary Ann went into a coma in the last stage before she died of an aneurysm caused from an over-dose of cocaine at age 45. Before Jeanne got to the hospital, she had called and given orders that Justin see his mother in the hospital. Jeanne said he needed to say goodbye to her. Her brothers followed Jeanne's wishes and Justin spent two hours with his mother.

When Jeanne arrived, she promised Mary Ann that she would take care of Justin. She knew Mary Ann would rest peaceably after that until she died.

Her brothers were overwhelmed with their sister's passing. After she died, Jeanne held the service in the chapel in the church of St. Augustine for Neal and Carol, Michael's wife, Justin, Sonny, and his wife Karen. While Michael was absent, the absence of son David and his live-in girlfriend/caretaker; filled the room. Carol never offered any explanation of the father Michael's absence, and no third party, not even mom, was informed as to why son David didn't come.

Carol had planned a luncheon after the funeral, but the family had trouble accepting her gift. Her previous inhospitable behavior towards all of them after she had married Michael was still very much in their thoughts. Neal made it very clear how he felt about her by not sitting down for lunch, choosing to go find a boat in St. Augustine's harbor to use to scatter Mary Ann's ashes. After the luncheon, everyone filed onto the boat with Jeanne holding the urn. She waited until they were out into open water, then opened the urn, poured them out carefully, but the breeze caught them and scattered them far and wide. Jeanne saves a small amount to send to some of Mary Ann's friends who had mentioned they wanted to honor Mary Ann with a memorial service, too.

Jeanne learned that Mary Ann had been vacationing on Jacksonville Beach before her early demise. She had left Justin with a friend and had just seen her father and friends before she died in the crack house. Jeanne was glad that Mary Ann had seen her father. Later, some unknown person called Michael and told him his daughter was dead and he needed to come get her. Michael rushed her to the hospital.

When Jeanne saw him in the hospital, he looked ill. Jeanne didn't know why he was sick. She told him that Mary Ann loved him more than he would ever know. Michael broke down and started to cry. Afterwards, he met with his sons, distraught. He achingly broke down with them, asking Mary Ann for forgiveness with his behavior as a disinterested father. His sons said that the room filled with a warm feeling, and they knew it was Mary Ann telling her father she was fine and forgiving him for his behavior.

Right after Mary Ann died, Jeanne had felt Mary Ann's presence and heard her say distinctly, "I'm sorry, Mom." At that moment, a warm and wonderful feeling filled the room.

She was teaching at the time in Lansing Michigan. Ten-year-old Justin had developed some serious behavior problems brought on by a lifetime of living with his drug dependent, divorced mother. At first, things went okay with Justin. Jeanne took him to interesting sporting events that she thought he would like, visited his school and met his teacher and tried in every way to make him feel comfortable. But gradually, as he started to develop hormones and was coming into his teenage years, he became belligerent and refused to mind Jeanne. It was hard for her not to have the firm hand of a father figure and she turned to the friendly custodian, Richard, for help.

Richard tried to take him in hand and steer Justin in the right direction, but he finally admitted that Justin was too much for him. Justin was thirteen and Jeanne was overwhelmed with his behavior. She began looking for help for him; social services, volunteer mentoring with an older boy, after school sports, but nothing worked. No one seemed the least bit interested in helping her or her grandson.

She called her two boys, David, and Neal, and asked for their advice. Neal suggested that she come and live at Lake Monticello, which was near where he and David lived in Palmyra, and he would try to help Justin.

Unhappily she decided to leave her teaching position and return to Virginia as Neal had suggested. She moved to Lake Monticello, Justin went to the public school, and it was a bad year for Justin. He didn't feel accepted, there were a lot of drugs being sold in school and Justin wasn't doing well educationally. Jeanne felt she was wasting her time and was too far out in the sticks to accomplish anything for herself.

She stuck it out for a year and moved back to Charlottesville where she knew people and had friends.

Remembering the year that 13-year-old Neal and 10-year-old David had gone to a military academy and done well, she toyed with the idea of sending Justin to one, too, but learned, even with a scholarship, she couldn't afford it. So, she sent him to public school and soon the school boys realized Justin had a little money, enough to buy drugs and they were only too happy to sell them to him. He became a user to hide from the pain he felt growing up with a drug-dependent mother. He also had

ADHD and Jeanne wondered if as a fetus he had ingested the drugs his mother was taking causing him harm.

In May 2003, another tragedy occurred in the Corrigan family. Michael died at age 69, only two years after his daughter, Mary Ann. Over two hundred people came to his funeral in Jacksonville. Neal went and handed out hundred-dollar bills to a lot of close friends because he said that was what his father would have done. The funeral was a social affair, something the south was good at.

Jeanne thought about Michael's family and their addictions. Every form of dependency had plagued the Corrigan's. Every one of the children and even their mother, Syd, were alcoholics. Michael 's father never missed his two double scotches every night, too. Even his father's side was full of uncles and aunts who were alcoholics.

Although she never thought much about it when she was married to Michael and fighting and fighting with him all the time, in later years, she had the distinct impression that she and Michael had planned their lifetime together long before they reincarnated, addictive genes and all. Her life would be consumed with all forms of addiction that she would have to deal with including Michael and their children's addiction to alcohol and drugs and her addiction to being rebellious.

Jeanne had hoped that spending her inheritance of eighty-five thousand dollars putting it in rehab programs would solve her children's addictive problems, but it didn't. The key to unlocking the problem of addiction had eluded her all her life. She asked herself, why didn't they want to stop their plunge so they could live and enjoy life?

One month later, the unspeakable happened, again. Their son, Neal, age 46, died from a perforated ulcer brought on by alcoholism. David had found his brother dead. Neal had been out on a date with a girl who lived across the street from Jeanne. Jeanne's only clue that something might happen was that Neal had complained that he felt awful and needed some milk. Neal knew what was wrong. He had a perforated ulcer. Peritonitis set in and killed him.

Jeanne asked herself many times after that, why wouldn't he go to a doctor and be treated for alcoholism? It almost seemed that he wanted to die. Why would he want that?

Distraught with the death of her second child, Jeanne reached out for help from her old friend, Kate. When Jeanne told Kate what had happened, Kate offered to come, be with her dear friend again and use her gourmet cooking skills to give Jeanne a much-needed boost. Kate cooked and cooked, pouring out her love to everyone with delicious meals for all of Neal's friends, and all the family who came to the funeral.

Facing Mary Ann's death had been impossible for Jeanne, and she had hidden her grief away, but found it easier to release her anguish and cry bitter tears for both Mary Ann and Neal.

Even a young man, Sally Vickers's son, came and praised Neal for all his kindness and help when he needed it. Gail and John Gillian drove all the way from West Palm Beach, Florida to be with Jeanne. They had been friends since Jeanne first moved to Charlottesville and John had taken a great interest in her children, all through the years, helping them into rehab programs. Jeanne's sister, Nell Leigh and her two daughters and Roberta, Neal's old girlfriend, came bringing many of their shared friends. His ex-wife, was there too, and brought his young daughter from New York and Jeanne's old friend, Mimi, gave a beautiful and touching service, bringing many people to tears when she closed with the same poem that Jeanne had read at Mary Anne's funeral.

Somehow, grieving for Mary Ann after she died had been impossible for Jeanne and she had hidden her grief away, but when Neal died, she found it easier to release her anguish and cry bitter tears for both Mary Ann and Neal.

Now, David was her only child and the remaining member of her family left. He and Jeanne had long talks after the funeral about the terrible toll drugs and alcohol had on their family. It was through their deaths that David opened to understanding that there was another dimension where his beloved sister and brother were there with his father, Michael. They discussed the fact that he could contact them, merely by thinking about them. To know that man's idea of death was false and that their souls never died was an inspiration to David and gave him courage to go on. Jeanne encouraged him to stop drinking.

Sonny was so grateful to Jeanne for providing a home for his younger brother, he continually called her and visited as often as possible. But because he was a young man trying to find his way, his visits were irregular.

Looking for a way to leave Charlottesville, a friend told her of a possible position at Life Stream, a metaphysical center in Roanoke asking for a position with them and they hired her. Twice a month, she drove to the center to work doing Aura Balancing with her clients. Another job working for Dr. Katz, wonderful holistic chiropractor, two days a week in Roanoke opened-up and Jeanne decided to take it. On her way to work every day, she passed a home that reminded her of Gerald Claire, her old boyfriend's home in Dade City when she was a child. She had a desire to see him again.

At the same time, she was preparing to be the Master of Ceremonies at a metaphysical conference in Johnson City, Tennessee. Jeanne fantasized seeing Gerald Claire out in the audience of the conference because she remembered that his family had moved to Tennessee when he was in grade school. It made her fantasy plausible.

However, it didn't happen, but a letter from an old friend, Charles Apperson from Dade City did come inviting her to a reunion at her old high school, Pasco High. Immediately, she thought, wouldn't it be fun if Claire came too?

She wrote and asked Charles if Claire was coming and he said, "No!"

Six months later, Charles forwarded a letter Claire had given him to send to her. In it was her graduation invitation and picture that he had kept for fifty years along with a letter saying he had missed her. He had always wondered what had become of her. His letter had no return or email address and no phone number.

Frustrated that she couldn't contact him, she tried to reach Charles to find out Claire's personal information from him, but he didn't respond for six months. When she finally heard from Charles, she asked for Claire's email address and was told that he would have to get Claire's permission before he could give it to her. Claire had obviously become a very private person.

The first letter that Claire wrote to her was sent through Charles to be forwarded to Jeanne. In it, he described incidents that had happened to her that she did not remember.

She was struck with his writing talent, amusing her with his way with words. He had kept in touch with many of their friends over the years and shared bits of their lives with her, too. He also wrote about the quaintness of Dade City and how lucky he was to have lived there.

From that formal communication, they began emailing each other daily in February 2007, while she was still living in Charlottesville. Through their emails they gradually discovered each other again. With every email to each other, they moved closer until they slowly fell in love, again. Gerald Claire confessed and shared the sordid details of his difficult marriage that he wanted to end but felt there were many personal reasons why he should stay including two darling granddaughters. However, he wrote beautiful love letters to Jeanne, and on one particular day, she received a letter from him pouring out his love for her in a history of his feelings for her over the years. He wrote:

Dear Jeanne,

This is the story of my life. I decided to leave out most of my chapters except for chapter one. It is a short chapter, covering only the first ten, plus two years of my life. So, I will be brief. It was during this brief span that I met the "girl of my dreams," and that is what sets the first chapter apart. It was not an auspicious meeting, yet one that I never quite got over. We were only twelve when the winds of change blew us in different directions. I felt lost. You gave me my first kiss. I saw you once again when we were seventeen. Again, the winds of fate prevailed, and we were blown in different directions. Again, I felt lost!

For the next six decades, I sauntered through life searching, always searching for something to make me whole. The sad part of this was that I didn't know what I was searching for. All I knew was to run, run and run some more! Well, run I did. Was I running in search of something to make me whole? Was I running from the situations that I alone had created? Or was I running from myself. I suppose that I will never know the answer to these questions.

Now that I am at the end of my chapters, I have stopped running. Why? Let me tell you of the wonderful ending to my life. The "girl of my dreams," sought me out after all these years. You came from nowhere to ask about my life. As we awkwardly felt each other out, you surmised that I had had a good life. Relatively speaking, I suppose that is true. A marriage of forty-nine years, three wonderful sons, five grandchildren and one great grandchild; these are things that story books are made of. Yet, there was a void in my life that could only be filled by one who had reached out and touched me, you.

We both knew immediately that we had touched each

other's very core. We dared not speak of it for fear we would drive it the other way. We spoke of being pen pals and then cheerleaders for each other. You see, we were both in denial of what was taking place. The girl of my dreams had been through three divorces and had lost two of her three children in untimely deaths. She was so hurt, so convinced that she could never find someone who would not criticize her or take advantage of her. She had never known anything else in her seventy years of living.

On the other hand, I had closed my heart and had resigned myself to dedicating the remainder of my life to my two darling granddaughters. They had become my passion, the anesthesia for making it through. I lived solely for them. They had become so precious to me. They were the closest beings to pure love that I had ever experienced until the girl of my dreams returned.

Where had she been all my life? She had been running against the winds just as I had been. She knew something was missing but had given up hope that it would come to her. She had learned years ago that God had endowed her with a wonderful spiritual gift of healing. She had set about dedicating the remainder of her days to helping others. She was so gifted that her reputation grew, and she continued to give, and give some more. She had become a vessel of the healing process for all who came to her. She gave, gave, and gave some more until her very lifeblood had almost been depleted.

When the girl of my dreams came back to me, I feared revealing my innermost thoughts of what had happened in the other chapters in my life. I cautiously drafted a lengthy letter telling her of the roads I had traveled. It was brutally honest and forthright. I held the letter for days contemplating how she would respond. Was I setting myself up for rejection? Would she think I was still holding on to a childhood fantasy? Would she think I had lost actually lost my seventy-year-old mind?

I named my letter, The Purge, mailed it and held my

breath. She responded immediately after receiving it with a letter with the opening words, Oh my love. I literally fell on my knees in relief. Could this be? The girl of my dreams cared for me. What was happening to my world? How could I possibly deal with this love that was surging through my body? I was scared. How could I handle this wonderful adventure and my marriage, too? Was this real or just a fantasy that would not go away?

The girl of my dreams reciprocated by revealing what had happened during all the chapters in her life. We were instantly bonded. Jeanne didn't realize it, but she was fast becoming a teacher/healer for someone who she had not seen or touched for nearly sixty years. Again, she was giving and giving without any expectation of anything in return. That was the nature of this woman, and she knew little else. By filling up everyone's vessel, perhaps someone would respond and give her a trickle of this thing called love. Up until now, she had been given abandonment instead.

I was mystified that anyone could not see the inner beauty of this woman who had been in my mind all my life. We had worked through the "fantasy" feeling we had for each other, and our love began to grow stronger day by day. We had begun to reach a comfort level that allowed us to express not only our love, but our concerns. Above all, we accepted each other as if we were true soul mates. I am hers; she is mine. I hurt for he, she hurts for me. I love her more than words can express she loves me back.

We now face the winter of our lives knowing that fate is not always kind. It is sometimes bitter. How many hapless souls can say that they did find the most wonderful person in the entire world to share the remainder of their lives. God has been kind to us by allowing two lost souls to finally experience the fullness of love as intended when he created us.

THANK YOU, JEANNE, FOR ALLOWING ME TO COME INTO YOUR LIFE AND FOR LOVING ME THE WAY YOU DO. REST

ASSURED THAT MY LOVE FOR YOU IS REAL AND WILL NOT
FADE WITH TIME.

      Peace. Always, Gerald

   Jeanne wrote

back:

   My Dearest Love,

First, I felt such freedom for both you and me when I read your letter. I also want to thank you for being the wonderful person you are and for what you have written about me. I feel so honored and appreciative that you are in my life and love me. Your love has brought to the surface many memories that I am putting together for the first time. Your talent with words brings out my feelings that I have evidently blocked until now. I wish I had that ability. I just love the way you write. This gift of creativity that has been given to you must be shared with the world.

Knowing that you will not criticize me for what I am going to share with you makes me feel very brave and secure. Some of the things that shaped me into the woman I am are what I must tell you.

In 1978, I went into counseling to discover why I had such angry feelings about my mother and how she had affected my life. Her emotional and mental abuse of me caused me to rebel against authority, sometimes to my detriment in my marriages, especially with Michael. Once I learned how she put me down and criticized everything that I did, my life changed. I no longer allowed people to abuse me, and I began looking carefully at all my relationships. Sometimes, however, I would slip back allowing it and it was always disastrous for me.

I finally stood up to her when I was older and the first time, I said I would not allow her to talk to me the way she was, I thought she was going to hit me. From then on for the next year and a half, I never let her get away with one nasty remark she tried to make to me. She finally stopped trying to bully me. I believe her bullying was the reason I let other girls bully me in my school. She also tried to make my half-sister dislike me and encouraged any unkind patterns of selfish behavior from Nell Leigh.

I have always had trouble setting my boundaries because I was always too frightened to do it when I was growing up. I was worried that people wouldn't like me if I stood up for myself.

I never really knew my father. As I look back, I feel he was very loving like you are. When I was at camp, my dad didn't write often but when he did, he never criticized me, he was very loving. I also believe he couldn't show his affection for me because of my mother. She would have made his life more miserable than it already was trying to please her. I was very proud of him when he was awarded the highest honor of a banker, being appointed to the Federal Reserve Board. I remember when he died the only thing my mother said was, she would triple the estate now that she was in charge.

Although I hope this will help you to understand me a little better, none of it matters anymore since you have come into my life. I just want to be with you and the rest in secondary. I have waited for you all my life and I feel you are with me. I would love to feel your arms around me right this second.

Finally, I want to say that we all have lessons to learn and tests to take in this lifetime whether we like it or not. We all work through our lessons in different ways with different teachers. Many of our teachers are harsh so we get the message. Even then we times, ignore the lesson they are trying to teach us. I also believe that the biggest lesson that anyone on this planet has to learn is to love themselves and set their boundaries. Loving themselves means taking care of themselves and not allowing anyone or anything to hurt them.

And now, after revealing more about me, I hope you will be your understanding self with what I have told you. I love you,

Gerald, and know that we will make a good team for the rest of our lives.

Peace, Jeanne

When he wrote back and thanked her for her honesty and love, she knew she was crazy in love with him. They planned their first meeting in over fifty years in July 2007 at the Hampton Inn in Roanoke.

The whole hotel knew that they had not seen each other in fifty years and were excited for them. Jeanne had told the staff that she was meeting the man of her dreams when she had investigated it for their meeting.

During July Gerald took his family on a trip and read Sylvia's Brown's book.

Jeanne moved to Roanoke in August 2007 to their future home. Gerald had matched her thousand dollars with his to secure the rental house, but she wasn't sure when he would be able to come to live with her. She was so grateful for his financial assistance because she wouldn't have been able to rent the house without his help. They were going to live there together! Jeanne couldn't believe it, but she reveled in her love for him and knew they would be happy.

When she thought about him, she felt they had many positive things in common besides their passion for each other. They both loved music and Gerald was an accomplished saxophone player. They also shared a spiritual bond and Jeanne helped to open him up. Their emails had touched on the idea of working together to help 'Born again Christians' understand the metaphysical belief system which was not a religion. Jeanne was overjoyed to think she would finally be married to someone who was interested in what she believed in and was willing to come from his 'Born again Christian' background and learn about her belief in the energy of the universe.

The day Jeanne moved in with her friends from Charlottesville and Covington helping, Gerald Claire arrived unannounced with some of his clothes and personal things. It surprised and delighted her and her friends to meet the love of her life.

The rest of the month, Gerald and Jeanne spent the time getting to know each other. It was then that Jeanne discovered about Gerald that she hadn't been aware of during their email courtship. He was an alcoholic!

When Gerald went back to Tennessee to sign the divorce papers, with the intention of marrying Jeanne, his children were waiting for him with an ultimatum. They said if he divorced their mother, he would never see his grandchildren again.

Making a painful decision, Gerald chose to resume his miserable life with his wife Josephine so he could have contact with his children and grandchildren.

He wrote to Jeanne about his change of heart, came back on a Saturday when Jeanne was working and packed up his things. When Jeanne got home, they sat down and talked about his future without her. It only took an hour for him to destroy all their hopes and dreams.

As Jeanne walked aimlessly through their home, she saw Gerald had left a personal item in each room for her to remember him. As the shock of his decision subsided and he had gone for good, Jeanne reassessed her feelings for the outcome. Perhaps, it was best in the long run for it to have turned out that way. To keep a good marriage intact, it's like caring for a garden. It takes continual attention to produce beautiful results. Maybe more than either of them had to give.

They kept in contact by email, but their lives were slowly separating as their feelings for each other cooled. Their dream was slowly evaporating into thin air as Gerald so eloquently wrote in his final letter to her.

YOU WERE THERE FOR A MOMENT AND THEN GONE,

CAPTURED ONLY IN MY DREAMS.

Where had she been for all my life? Where else, but traveling the same highways, carrying the same burdens, looking for something that she knew little of. She was little different than I. In fact, she had resigned herself to an existence that made her void. Her losses had been heavy, much heavier than mine. She had one thing that I didn't, the drive to make something different happen in her life. She had served others for so long that she almost lost herself. But she had a tiny spark that allowed her to reach into the night and say, "Hello, again."

She will never fade from my dreams even though I cannot leave my world. I will always love you, Jeanne. Peace, Gerald

Jeanne's response was slow because she needed time to make her final letter to her momentary love.

My Dearest Love,

I don't know exactly what you want from me, but I am going to answer you with what I feel, now. I, too, spent most of my life running, just like you admitted in your email. I also tried to force things to happen the way I thought they should because I felt I was supposed to. I only had disasters happen as a result of my flawed thinking.

I didn't run most of my life until slowly a belief system that made sense to me appeared in my life. It taught us to let things happen naturally. It also told me to follow that wee small voice from within, my intuition, and allow things to happen when the timing was right. The timing for us to be together was not right.

For a long time, things were not working for me. I was not happy with my life, felt tired, depressed, and living a life that didn't have much meaning for me. My relationships with men had been disastrous, so bad I decided to not try anymore.

When I was forced to turn and feel the unconditional love that Spirit and legions of guides, teachers, and angels provided from beyond the veil, a miracle happened. I was filled with hope and wish to help others. I also learned that I had no control over anyone or anything in the Universe, except myself. That was a big lesson.

For a long time, I moved all over the country, learning many different healing techniques. But it was a way of not facing my own problems. I was healing others, but not myself.

When my two children died, I spent weeks and months with my son, David trying to heal. As I gradually returned to work, I had a premonition that there was someone out there that was waiting for me. Not until I received my picture and a letter from you, did I know who it was. All through the years, your memory had haunted me. During those years of driving to Tennessee to run the conference, I kept wondering if you were still in Tennessee. I also wondered if you felt anything for me after all those years. I kept praying to Spirit that I would find you to put this urgent feeling to rest. It had become an obsession for me. I wanted to know where you lived, if you were married, and had dozens of other questions about you inside me just waiting to be answered.

However, I used my old tactics of pushing to get what I wanted, and I wanted you, but it didn't work. All I got was frustration. I finally asked myself, how can I contact you? I knew I had to clear my energy field to get anywhere with my quest. I worked hard using all my healing techniques and patterns to help me be able to reach you. Why did I have my burning need to find you? An astrologer had told me you were my twin flame. It only confirmed my feeling that there was an underlying love between us that came from our hearts and souls and was being awakened, subdued for many years. I felt as if there were great hands guiding me and directing me to find you. But accompanying this feeling was a nameless fear that something might happen. But that didn't stop me.

I was forced to deal with this overwhelming feeling of love and drive that I didn't understand, but wanted to so deeply that I would cry and feel I would never be allowed to have you. I will never forget how I felt when your letter came, and you told me how much you had loved me through the years. I knew this was the love that I had been waiting for all of my life.

I prayed and prayed that whatever happened would be for the highest good and we would not hurt anyone. If we were to be together, I asked Spirit to help us make it happen. I also prayed to be led to do what we were supposed to do when we are together. An astrologer told me that we are twin flames that were together many eons ago and are here again to change the lives of many others for the betterment of the Universe.

Thank you for what you gave me while we had our brief interlude together. You opened my heart, my creativity and changed my life. I am deeply grateful to you and will be forever. I love you, my darling with my whole being, but I want you to know that my faith in Spirit has been strengthened and I will be alright.

Although Jeanne had promised not to write to Gerald again, she found she had to write one more letter before she said goodbye.

Dearest Gerald,

You said in one of your letters that you felt our relationship was a blessing and a curse. You also said that you knew I felt that way, too. Sweetheart, I want you to know that in this entire year of our love affair, with everything we have been through, I have never, never thought of our relationship as a curse. I am so thankful for God, Holy Spirit, guides and guardian angels for guiding us this past year. It was meant to be, and you have given me more love and acceptance in a year than I have had in my whole life.

I have written at least ten letters to you and never sent them because of worrying that I was overstepping my boundaries. But I'm finally convinced that I need to tell you how I saw your marriage. If I can make it better for you in the situation you have chosen to live in, then I have done the right thing. Perhaps, that was one of the reasons we had our brief time together.

I feel that there is a part of you that doesn't see or understand what you have been dealing with because you are too close to the situation. Your grandchildren are just an excuse not to face the issues you have with Josephine. If you had been honest with your son, Chris, about the way Josephine treats you, both physically and mentally, he would not have forbidden you to see your grandchildren even if you were married to me.

You have a love hate relationship with your wife, I saw it a lot this year. The minute Josephine would get mellow, you would feel sorry and extremely guilty. You have spent fifty years looking for Josephine's acceptance of you the same way you tried to get your father's approval. She apparently doles out a meager amount to you sometimes and you convince yourself that you are satisfied. Staying with her gives you a sense of security or safety almost like the prisoner who is set free feels when he returns to jail for some small infraction of the system. Your children treat you the same way as Josephine. I hope you can teach them all unconditional love. Then perhaps, you will find some harmony with your wife so you both can live in peace instead of conflict.

When I told you I took a year out of my life to spend with you, I meant it in the most positive sense. It was the happiest year of my life and there was never a moment that I didn't learn something from you and was totally happy with you. It was wonderful to have you as my friend who was accepting of me, never angry and always there to listen and discuss our different views.

You made me feel totally loved and it was the most beautiful feeling I have ever experienced. I was able to give my love back to you in a way I've never been able to do in all of my relationships.

Thanks, you for loving me for who I am and not for who you wanted me to be. Thank you for teaching me how to express myself through writing. Thank you for your loving letters, poems, and wonderful conversations. Thank you for your kindness, thoughtfulness and generosity. The money you gave me after the operations, when I desperately needed was a Godsend. And finally, thank you for just being you. It is sad to say goodbye, but it is as it is supposed to be.

I love you Gerald Claire, more than words can express and from the depth of my heart, mind, body and soul. Thank you for a wonderful year. Happy Valentine's Day. You will always be my valentine. Peace, always, Jeanne.

My religion is simple, It is kindness. Dalai Lama

My World is My Faith

EPILOGUE

2007-2014

Jeanne

While Jeanne was grieving for Gerald, in another nearby town, a lonely man named David was reeling from a foolish marriage to a woman that turned out to be a drug addict.

As he told Jeanne later, "I was lonely after being married all those years. I never dreamed my first wife of 36 years would kill herself. I had proposed marriage to my first wife, two weeks after meeting her. I tried that quick proposal thing with the second wife, and it did not work out. The woman who came along after my first wife passed, needed a 'helping hand up'. After marriage I learned that I had married a Crack addict."

"It's called rebound. I know all about that. I did it twice" replied Jeanne.

"You did?" He asked, delighted not to be the only one who had made mistakes. "I'm so glad I found your healing advertisement on the internet.

"When you called," Jeanne said, "You sounded nice, and I needed the money."

"I liked you the minute I met you, only I wasn't sure of myself after my disastrous marriage. You gave me a great healing. I would have come a lot more, but twice was all I could afford."

"I wondered where you went. I figured you had other things to do and when you hadn't called after a month or two, I thought I'd never see you again."

"I know, four months is a long time, but I was trying to recover from that gal. But when you said yes, you'd go out for dinner with me, I was really happy.'"

"I was hungry. I also wanted to get to know you."

"And look at us now, after knowing each other for seven years, we're finally going to live together."

"I hope we can work things out, so we don't step on each other's toes," Jeanne said, with a concerned look on her face.

"We will," David said, hopefully. We just have to make some space for each other."

"I will say this, David, our belief systems are the closest of any of my husbands or boyfriends.

"When you told me you were a Reiki teacher, David, I was sure that our metaphysical worlds were compatible."

"I have watched you heal people for seven years and I know we are very close," David replied, but I've always wondered what you meant when you said your world was your faith."

"I'll be glad to tell you. Very few people have ever asked me that. I really believe that I am here for a purpose and to fulfill a mission. I had to come in and learn what I have learned to be able to help the people I help, today. Every part of my life; starting with the childhood abuse that I suffered, the wild parties, the drinking, the sex, going through hell with my kids, losing two children, and three divorces have been instrumental in my understanding of everyone who has come to me for help. All the people who have come to me have suffered some of the same things I have, except for heavy sexual abuse. Up until then, I didn't think I could help them on that subject because that had never happened to me."

"But I was wrong. Do you remember David when I

had the magenta problem?"

"I do. I couldn't believe that the printer wouldn't print the manual that you needed to print. Every page was covered with magenta ink. You tried a second printer, and it did the same thing. On the third little old printer that I found in the basement; you were able to print the whole thing except for page 96. You tried to print it three times.',

"I realized, David, that magenta is a color of etheric origin. It is the color of physical energy which enters the physical body. Without it, illness occurs. And just now when I tried to print something three times and it wouldn't print that page it told me that something was wrong. Every little thing has a meaning, David, and I knew Spirit wanted me to learn something. That's why I went back to the master manual and read that on page 96, sexual abuse was discussed. You see, Spirit was showing me that I needed to delve into my childhood and find sexual abuse in my life.

" Jeanne, you really are psychic."

"That's not all. I did a lot of meditating on the subject and remembered a lot more about the times my mother's good friend's son who was fourteen at the time had fondled me. I was five or six and slightly in awe of him. I didn't know how to say no or tell my mother. She wouldn't have believed me. He never hurt me, but I didn't like it." "Wow, you learned all that by meditating?"

"Yes, Spirit always answers me."

"Of course, and it made the regression much better."

"What did you learn?"

"I learned that I gave Michael faith, both when I was a slave on his plantation and when I was married to him during this lifetime."

"Maybe, I should go and find out about me."

"It wouldn't be a bad idea."

"One of the reasons I've decided to let us live together is the way you want your freedom, and you respect mine. You also worry about my business and try to help me keep this place up."

"You also aren't an alcoholic. That's a big thing for me. Every man in my life, except for my father, has been one or close to it."

"And the last and most important thing of all is you aren't a womanizer, and you are a wonderful lover. I have never had such a great sex life as I have had with you. It's wonderful every time."

David smiled a sexy smile and said, "That's what make us so good together. I need a woman who loves to make love because so do I."

"Let's get to work, now. We must clean out my basement and make room for your things. Life is going to be easier for both of us by joining forces and someday, you can take care of me, and I will take care of you when we get old."

"You're right. We can't rely on our kids. They have their own problems," David answered, emphatically.

But David, there is one teensy little problem I have with you," Jeanne said, giving him a wry look.

"What's that?" He answered a little too quickly

To Be Continued …

ABOUT THE AUTHOR

Dr. Jeanne Greening

On June 25th 2020, Jeanne received her Doctorate and PhD in Natural Medicine from International Quantum University for Integrative Medicine at age 83.

Dr. Jeanne's workshops:

Greening Healing Technique

Patterns

Color and Sound

Pendulum

Emotion
To be released soon ...

Made in the USA
Middletown, DE
14 September 2023

38481515R00106